The Wind at Work

An Activity Guide to Windmills

Gretchen Woelfle

CHICAGO
REVIEW
PRESS

Library of Congress Cataloging-in-Publication Data
Woelfle, Gretchen.
The wind at work : an activity guide to windmills / by Gretchen
Woelfle.––1st ed.
p.   cm.
Includes bibliographical references (p. 137–38).
Summary: An introduction to windmills and their advantages as renewable energy
providers, with activities for understanding some of the principles of wind.
ISBN 1-55652-308-4
1. Windmills–History–Juvenile literature. [1. Windmills.]
I. Title
TJ823.W64 1997
621.4'5–DC20   96-24560
                                                                          CIP
                                                                          AC

Photographs on the front cover from upper right corner and clockwise: "The Mill at Wijk," by Dutch artist Jacob van Ruisdael (1628–1682) courtesy of the Royal Netherlands Embassy; stone tower mill at Palma de Mallorca courtesy of Tourist Office of Spain, Los Angeles; wind turbines courtesy of Zond Corporation; large green smock mill on the Zaan River in the Netherlands courtesy of Netherlands Board of Tourism; Western windmill photograph by Bob Popeck, Batavia, Il., windmill owned by the City of Batavia.

Interior design by Sean O'Neill

© 1997 by Gretchen Woelfle
All rights reserved
First edition
Published by Chicago Review Press, Incorporated
814 North Franklin Street
Chicago, Illinois 60610
ISBN 1-55652-308-4
Printed in the United States of America
5 4 3 2 1

To my mother and father, Ruth and Bud Woelfle

Acknowledgments

This book could not have been written without the generous help of many people.

I offer special thanks to Paul Gipe who read and critiqued the manuscript and shared his knowledge and his photo archive with me. The following people have also generously contributed to this book: Dr. T. Lindsay Baker, Diane Hamilton, Lynn Harrison, Jerry Leeds, Jessica Maier and the American Wind Energy Association, Jim Owen, Peter Tailer, and Stanley Zaminski.

Aura Woelfle, Wilfred Rosdorff, and Gebrandt de Vries, President De Hollandsche Molen, served as translators and helpful ambassadors on my research trip to the Netherlands.

Caroline Arnold, Sherrill Kushner, Alexis O'Neill, and Kathleen Thorne-Thomsen offered encouragement and advice during the long gestation of this book. Lisa Rosenthal-Hogarth has been a meticulous and most congenial editor.

I am grateful to Cottages of Hedgebrook and the Ragdate Foundation for writers' residencies that gave me time and space to work.

The following people offered special help in gathering illustrations for the book: Katherine Blood, Library of Congress; Askov Højskole; Bruce Loeschen; Karen Lougheed, Kenetech Windpower, Inc.; Mary McCann, Zond Corporation; Loraine Netto and Saskia Brandt, Netherlands Board of Tourism; Robert Popeck and the Batavia Historical Society; David Spera; and Judith Friso, De Zaansche Molen.

Finally, I want to thank Alice and Clea Woelfle-Erskine for reading the manuscript, quality-testing the activities and giving me their fiercely candid impressions. Peter Erskine, once again, has provided the intellectual and personal support that I cherish in our lifelong partnership.

Contents

ONE

HARNESSING WIND POWER THROUGH TIME 1

Activities 7

TWO

ANCIENT WIND MACHINES 11

Activities 15

THREE

WINDMILLS IN EUROPE ACROSS THE CENTURIES 21

Activities 30

FOUR

A WINDMILLER'S LIFE 35

Activities 45

FIVE

ALL-AMERICAN WINDMILLS 49

Activities 57

SIX

INVENTORS AND COWBOYS WORK THE WIND 65

Activities 73

SEVEN

A NEW KIND OF WINDMILL 77

Activities 83

EIGHT

WINDMILLS TODAY 87

Activities 95

NINE

FULFILLING THE PROMISE 101

Activities 113

WHERE TO FIND WINDMILLS 117
RESOURCE LISTING 125
   Renewable Energy and Wind Energy Groups 125
   Student Environmental Groups 125
   General Environmental Groups 126
   Historical Associations 127
WINDMILL CAREERS 129
GLOSSARY 131
PICTURE KEY TO WINDMILLS 134
BIBLIOGRAPHY 137
INDEX 139
ABOUT THE AUTHOR 145

CHAPTER ONE

Harnessing Wind Power Through Time

Night fell on the flatlands of Holland. The wind howled, rain slashed to earth, and waves broke higher and higher on the beach. Flashes of lightning revealed a high wall of earth built to hold back the sea. Waves crashed against this dike, throwing water to the fields beyond and washing away parts of the dike.

The Dutch called the sea the Waterwolf, and tonight the Waterwolf was on the prowl, trying to steal their lands. All night long flickering lanterns moved along the top of the dike as villagers kept watch. If the dikes broke, the Waterwolf would swallow their farms and homes.

By morning, the rain subsided and the wind dropped. The storm was over. The dikes had held. Tired Dutchmen stumbled home to bed.

But there was no rest for the windmillers. All night they had worked the windmills to pump water from the overflowing canals back out to sea. Now they had to drain the flooded fields to save the crops. For days and nights, giant windmill sails would turn–pumping and pumping until the fields were dry. The wind that nearly destroyed the land would now help to save it.

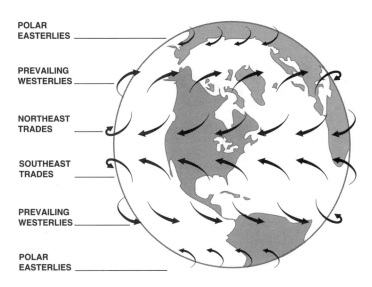

POLAR EASTERLIES

PREVAILING WESTERLIES

NORTHEAST TRADES

SOUTHEAST TRADES

PREVAILING WESTERLIES

POLAR EASTERLIES

Wind is created by the sun as it warms the earth unevenly. Lands near the equator get more sun than those near the poles. Summer brings more sun than winter. Warm air expands and rises and cool air rushes in to take its place. This air movement is the wind. The drawing shows the usual, or prevailing, winds in different parts of the earth. *Kristin Brivchik*

The History of Wind Power

Wind is created by the sun as it warms the earth unevenly. Warm air expands and rises. Cool air rushes in to take its place. This air movement is what we call the wind.

For more than a thousand years people have harnessed the wind with windmills. People used the wind to propel sailboats on the water long before they built windmills on land. Billowing sails filling with wind replaced the hard work of men rowing and paddling. Eventually, wind-powered machines moved on land and saved a lot of heavy labor. The wind-filled windmill sails then turned a shaft, wheels, gears, and finally, millstones, water pumps, or other machines. Before the invention of windmills and water mills, men or animals turned heavy *millstones* by trudging around and around in a circle, hour after hour, day after day, crushing grain to make flour. It was mind-numbing, body-breaking work.

Along the seacoast the land and the air above the land warm up quicker than the water. All day long this warm air rises and cool sea breezes blow from the ocean to the land. *Kristin Brivchik*

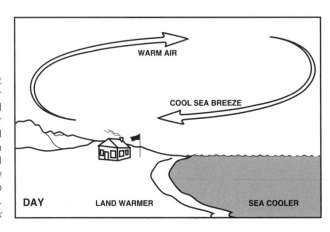

WARM AIR

COOL SEA BREEZE

DAY   LAND WARMER   SEA COOLER

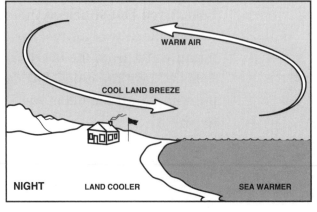

WARM AIR

COOL LAND BREEZE

NIGHT   LAND COOLER   SEA WARMER

In the evening the land cools off quicker, and the ocean remains warmer. Warm ocean air rises and a cooler land breeze blows out to sea. *Kristin Brivchik*

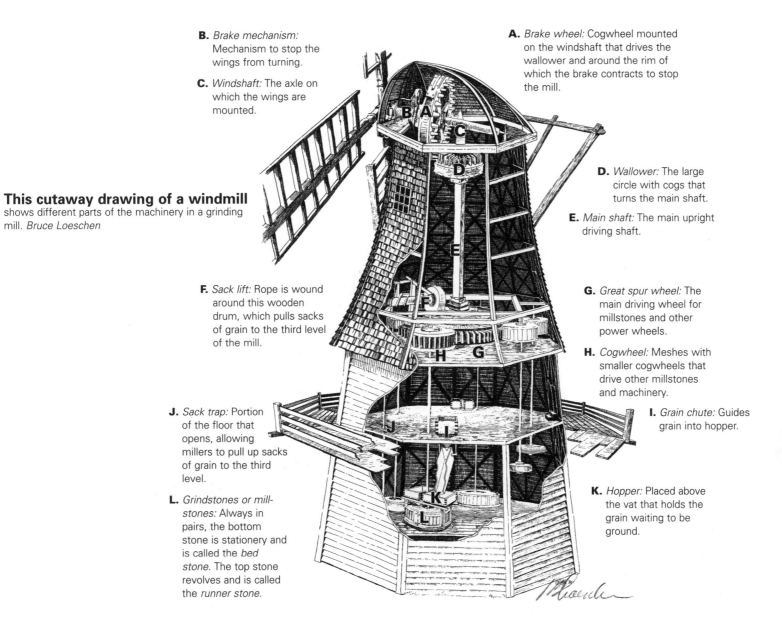

B. *Brake mechanism:* Mechanism to stop the wings from turning.

C. *Windshaft:* The axle on which the wings are mounted.

A. *Brake wheel:* Cogwheel mounted on the windshaft that drives the wallower and around the rim of which the brake contracts to stop the mill.

D. *Wallower:* The large circle with cogs that turns the main shaft.

E. *Main shaft:* The main upright driving shaft.

This cutaway drawing of a windmill shows different parts of the machinery in a grinding mill. *Bruce Loeschen*

F. *Sack lift:* Rope is wound around this wooden drum, which pulls sacks of grain to the third level of the mill.

G. *Great spur wheel:* The main driving wheel for millstones and other power wheels.

H. *Cogwheel:* Meshes with smaller cogwheels that drive other millstones and machinery.

J. *Sack trap:* Portion of the floor that opens, allowing millers to pull up sacks of grain to the third level.

I. *Grain chute:* Guides grain into hopper.

K. *Hopper:* Placed above the vat that holds the grain waiting to be ground.

L. *Grindstones or millstones:* Always in pairs, the bottom stone is stationery and is called the *bed stone*. The top stone revolves and is called the *runner stone*.

The wind is not a perfect source of energy. It can be steady or gusty. It can change direction in a few seconds. It can grow to the force of a hurricane or die completely. Scientists can predict daily and seasonal wind patterns, but these patterns won't tell if or how much the wind will blow tomorrow afternoon. Even so, the wind has been reliable enough for many uses through the centuries.

Like the wind itself, *windmills* have come and gone.

From A.D. 1200 to 1900, windmills were the most powerful machines in Europe. They ground grain, pumped water, pressed oil, sawed wood, and performed many other tasks. In the 1800s windmills were replaced by steam engines. Only nine hundred Dutch windmills remain out of ten thousand that stood two hundred years ago. In America, six million windmills pumped water on the dry Western plains until the 1940s when electric and gasoline engines did away

The Mill at Wijk is by Dutch artist Jacob van Ruisdael (1628–1682). The 1600s were the golden age of Dutch windmills and landscape painting. *Royal Netherlands Embassy*

with most of them. Today a new kind of windmill turns in the wind.

Many people think of Dutch models when they think of windmills, but windmills come in many shapes and sizes. Ancient Persian-style mills looked like revolving doors. Modern *wind turbines* look like giant airplane propellers. All can harness a powerful energy source to work for us.

Wind Power Today

Thousands of wind turbines stand in the deserts and hills of California today. Thousands more are scattered across Canada, Europe, and the rest of the world. They are new versions of an old idea.

From far away, wind turbines look like toy pinwheels that catch the sunlight as they spin. Up close, these pinwheel giants stand on one-hundred-foot towers with whirling blades up to one hundred feet in diameter. A generator behind the blades converts wind energy to electricity. Underground cables carry electric currents to power lines that feed the electricity to nearby towns and cities.

Clean, Renewable Energy Source

Wind power is a renewable source of energy, so we will never run out of it. It's clean, safe, and free for all to use.

Currently, most of the energy we use comes from burn-

The hills in Altamont Pass, in California, are covered with 6,500 wind turbines—the largest wind farm in the world. *Kenetech Windpower, Inc.*

ing coal, oil, and natural gas. These are called *fossil fuels*. When these fuels burn, gases like carbon dioxide, nitrogen oxides, and sulfur compounds escape into the air. The gases react with sunlight to create smog. They mix with water vapor in the clouds and fall to earth as *acid rain*. They also trap heat in our atmosphere and cause *global warming*. All these conditions are harmful to forests, crops, wildlife, and human life.

Wind power is a clean, economical energy source that can help reduce environmental pollution. Wind turbines could produce 10 percent of America's electrical power by the year 2000. This would save about 900,000 tons of coal, oil, and gas from going up in smoke every year.

Wind power is found in more places around the globe than fossil fuels. It is a clean, *renewable energy* that we will never use up. Some people discovered this a thousand years ago. Others don't know about it yet. But whether you've heard it or not, there's good news in the wind.

José Mascurel and his family pose proudly near the windmill on their ranch in Hollywood, California, in the 1880s. *Seaver Center for Western History Research, Los Angeles County Museum of Natural History*

COMPARE ELEMENT TEMPERATURES

Goal *Understand temperature patterns that affect the wind.*

Materials

2 plastic buckets of the same size

Water

Earth

3 outdoor thermometers

Notebook

Pencil

1 piece of graph paper

3 markers of different colors

Ruler

Directions

Fill one bucket with earth and the other bucket with water. Place a thermometer in each bucket. Place the buckets side by side outdoors. Place the third thermometer on the ground nearby to measure the air temperature. Make sure you place the buckets and thermometers where the sun can shine on them for part of each day.

Use the notebook to record your observations three times a day. For each observation, record the day of the week, time of day, the name of the element (water, earth, or air), the temperature reading on the thermometer, and the weather conditions. Record your observations for three days.

Day	Time	Element	Temperature	Condition
Monday	morning	water	76 degrees	sunny but cloudy
Monday	morning	earth	78	same
Monday	morning	air	77	same
Monday	afternoon	water	82	sunny
and so on . . .				

At the end of your three days of observation, create a chart like the one shown on page 8. Write in a temperature range on the vertical axis and the days on the horizontal axis leaving enough room to record your three daily observations. Use a different color marker to record your observations for each element. Place a dot in the spot where the day of the week and time intersect with the recorded temperature. Once you've recorded all your observations, use a ruler to connect these dots.

Results

What element has the highest temperature—water, earth, or air—in the morning? Afternoon? Evening?

Which element heats up the most during the day?

Which element cools down the most at night?

Which element shows the least temperature change during the day?

What does this tell you about the relative temperature of the oceans, earth, and atmosphere? How might these temperature differences affect wind patterns?

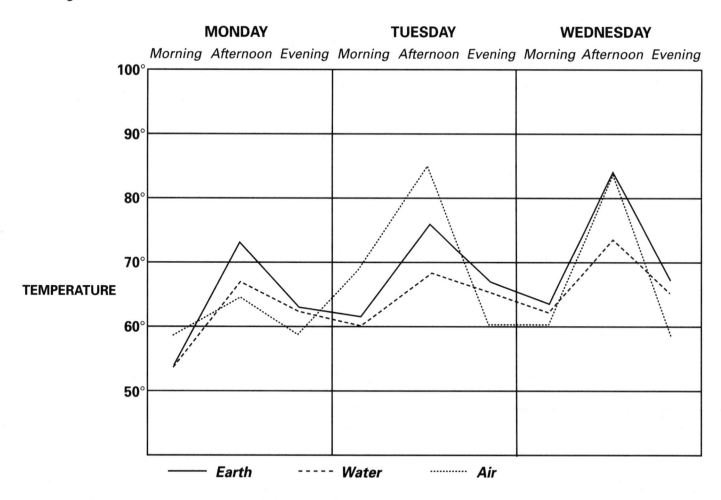

| MONDAY | | | TUESDAY | | | WEDNESDAY | | |

Morning Afternoon Evening Morning Afternoon Evening Morning Afternoon Evening

——— **Earth**   - - - - - **Water**   ·········· **Air**

LEARN HOW TEMPERATURE AFFECTS WIND

Goal *Observe the flow of air in a warm and cool environment.*

Materials

1 2-foot piece aluminum foil

1 small piece molding clay

1 thick candle, 4 inches tall

Matchbook

2 small wooden blocks, 1 or 2 inches thick

1 empty soup can, label and
both ends removed

1 sharp knife

1 piece heavy cotton string, 3 inches long
(Don't use nylon string!)

Directions

(Adult help suggested.)

Spread the aluminum foil on top of a table. Secure the candle to the foil with clay. Light the candle. Place 2 wooden blocks on opposite sides of the candle. Carefully place the can over the candle and resting on top of the 2 blocks. The candle flame should not show above the can. (If the candle is too tall, blow it out and cut it at the bottom so it will fit inside the can.)

Light the end of the string over the sink, then quickly blow out the flame. The string should smoke. Hold the smoking string 2 inches above the candle flame. Notice the temperature above the candle. What happens to the smoke?

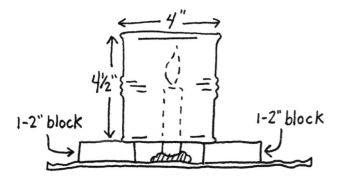

While the string continues to smoke, hold it beside the candle, about a foot away. Notice the temperature now. What happens to the smoke? Finally, hold the string near the table top, about ½ inch from the edge of the can. What happens to the smoke? How can you explain this?

Results

If our atmosphere were all the same temperature, air wouldn't move. However, sunlight warms our atmosphere just like a candle warms the air around it. The warm air rises, and the cooler air moves in to take its place. So, when you hold the string directly above the candle, the smoke rises. When you hold the string a foot away from the heat source, the smoke drifts because the air surrounding the string is not as warm. Finally, when you hold the string close to the bottom of the tin can, the smoke is drawn up under the can and rises because the smoke moves in the direction of the warmer air.

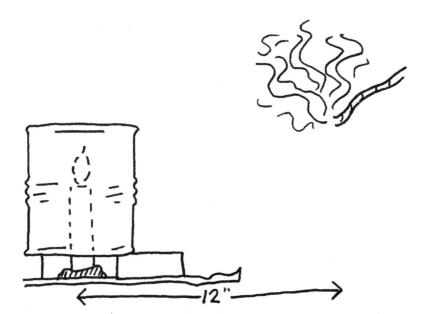

CHAPTER TWO

Ancient Wind Machines

Before people invented windmills they found other ways to harness the wind. Sails on boats carried mariners faster and farther than before. Four thousand years ago men in large sailing canoes explored the South Pacific. They found their way by watching the wind, stars, and ocean currents as they sailed from one small island to another across hundreds of miles of open ocean. In Egypt, graceful *dhows* have sailed down the Nile River for five thousand years. By 450 B.C. Phoenician sailors had traveled beyond the Mediterranean, north to Britain and south along the west coast of Africa.

Kites in the Wind

Kites are another way that the wind has been used for exploration. More than two thousand years ago, the Chinese began flying kites. They flew them in battle to signal their troops. On Kite Day they sent kites aloft, asking the sky gods to send good fortune in the coming year.

Benjamin Franklin began experimenting with kites as a boy. One day he floated on his back while his kite pulled him more than a mile across a lake. Since his kite would not carry him back against the wind, he paid a smaller boy a few pennies to tote his clothes from one shore to another.

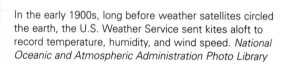

In the early 1900s, long before weather satellites circled the earth, the U.S. Weather Service sent kites aloft to record temperature, humidity, and wind speed. *National Oceanic and Atmospheric Administration Photo Library*

In 1752 Franklin flew a kite during a thunderstorm to prove that lightning contained electricity. He tied a key to the end of a silk kite string before sending it aloft. When lightning did strike his kite, he felt a slight electrical shock. He was lucky that his kite string remained fairly dry or his experiment would have been much more shocking. A Russian professor was killed a year later when he repeated Franklin's experiment with a wet kite string.

Scientists continued to use kites into the 1900s. Wilbur and Orville Wright designed and flew giant box kites. These experiments helped them invent the first successful airplane in 1903. From 1898 to 1933, the U.S. Weather Service sent kites aloft to record temperature, humidity, and wind speed.

In 1752 Benjamin Franklin used a kite to prove that lightning contained a massive electrical charge. *Library of Congress Prints and Photographs USZ62-1433*

Wind Furnaces

Archaeologists in the early 1990s found evidence to suggest that people living in Sri Lanka in the A.D. 700s used the wind to smelt (separate) metal from rock ore in an unexpected way. Traditionally, smelting furnaces are tall, narrow structures. People fan the furnace with a *bellows* to make the fire burn very hot–hot enough to melt metal. But in Sri Lanka, they dug large crescents near the top of steep mountainsides. Each July and August monsoon winds blew across the Indian Ocean, up the slopes, and into these crescent-shaped furnaces. Winds of twenty-five to thirty mph rushed into the furnaces and created a mini-tornado. Charcoal fires inside the furnace reached at least 2200°F (1200° C), hot enough to smelt iron or steel.

Gill Juleff, the British archaeologist in charge of the excavations says, "these furnaces break all the rules about smelting furnaces, yet we're sure they were used for making iron, and perhaps steel." Moslem armies invaded Sri Lanka during that time, and iron and steel were probably used for weapons as well as farming tools.

Around A.D. 950 the ancient Persians constructed a windmill by fastening bundles of reeds to a frame that rotated as the wind blew. They built walls around it to create a "wind tunnel" that would increase the force of the wind. *Sandia National Laboratory*

Persian Windmills

We first hear of windmills from traveling Arab geographers around A.D. 950. They visited the high desert plains of Seistan in ancient Persia, near the present Iran-Afghanistan border. There, a hot gale force wind blew from June through September. It was called "the wind of 120 days, the wind that killed cows."

People in Seistan built windmills that resembled modern revolving doors enclosed on two sides. The wind entered on one side, twirled the doors around, and exited on the other side. Attached to millstones, the windmills ground corn into meal. Connected to a pump, they raised water from underground wells to irrigate the parched land. The advantage of this windmill was that it worked no matter which way the wind blew. However, the wind only pushed against one door at a time, so only one-fourth of the windmill was using the wind at any given moment.

Windmills on the Move

Legend has it that in the 1200s the Mongolian armies of Genghis Khan captured Persian windmill builders and took them to China to build irrigation windmills. Persian-style windmills also spread westward through the Middle East. In Egypt they were used to grind sugar cane.

Centuries later, European settlers in the West Indies hired Egyptians to plant sugar cane and build windmills to grind it. It was in this way that a few ancient Persian–style windmills reached the New World.

MAKE A WIND SOCK AND WIND VANE

Wind socks are used in airports to show which direction the wind is blowing.

Goal *Make a wind sock and wind vane and learn how they work.*

Materials

1 nylon knee sock or 1 knee-high hose 15–18 inches long

1 12-ounce Styrofoam cup

1 3/16-inch wooden dowel, 3 feet long

2 straight plastic straws, 8 inches long (not the flexible kind)

1 1/4-inch washer

1 pushpin

1 sheet construction paper

Tools

Scissors

Pencil

Masking tape

White glue

Ruler

Compass

Directions

WIND SOCK

(Adult help suggested.)

1. Use the scissors to cut off the toe of the sock or the knee-high hose so that it is open at each end.

2. Cut out the bottom of the Styrofoam cup. Using a sharp pencil, bore a hole in the cup, just below the raised rim. This hole should be big enough for the 3/16-inch dowel to fit through. Bore another hole directly opposite the first one.

Use a sharp pencil to bore a hole in the Styrofoam cup just below the raised rim. Make a second hole directly across from the first one.

3. Stretch the wide end (knee end) of the sock or hose over the bottom of the cup up to the raised rim. Tape the sock or hose onto the rim by securing it with 1 long piece of tape. Reinforce it with 4 small pieces of tape around the rim.

4. Use scissors to snip holes in the sock or hose where the cup holes are located.

WIND SOCK POLE

1. Push the pushpin through the top end of the dowel as far as it will go. Then twist and remove the pushpin. (This hole will be needed for the next stage when you make your wind vane.)

2. Slide the wind sock onto the dowel through the 2 holes, leaving 1 inch free at the top.

3. Slide the ¼-inch washer up the pole until it rests just below the Styrofoam cup. Wrap a piece of tape around the pole several times just underneath the washer until it is thick enough to hold the washer in place. The washer will prevent the wind sock from sliding down the pole.

4. Wrap another strip of tape around the top end of the dowel just above the wind sock to keep it from sliding off the top of the pole.

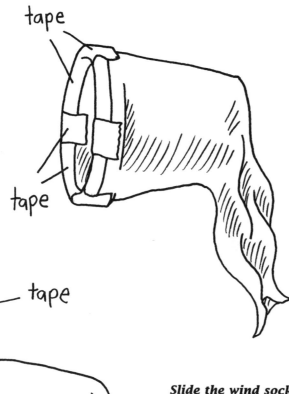

tape

tape

tape

tape

washer

Pull the sock or hose over the cup, from the bottom/narrower end up, and secure with tape. This is your wind sock. Use scissors to rip holes in the sock or hose where the cup holes are located.

Slide the wind sock onto the dowel through the 2 holes. Place the washer directly below the cup. Wrap tape around the pole directly above the cup and just below the washer to secure.

WIND VANE

1. Carefully cut ¼-inch slits in each end of the
   straws. Cut 4 small 1 by 1-inch squares of construction paper. Mark each square of construction paper with compass direction N, S, E, or
   W. Dab a drop of white glue on each side of
   the paper and slip one piece between each pair
   of slits on all 4 ends of the 2 straws. Place N
   and S on the 2 ends of 1 straw; E and W on the
   other, just like the compass points. Be sure that
   the paper is horizontal. Dab more glue on the
   spots where the paper meets the straw to
   secure. Allow this to dry.

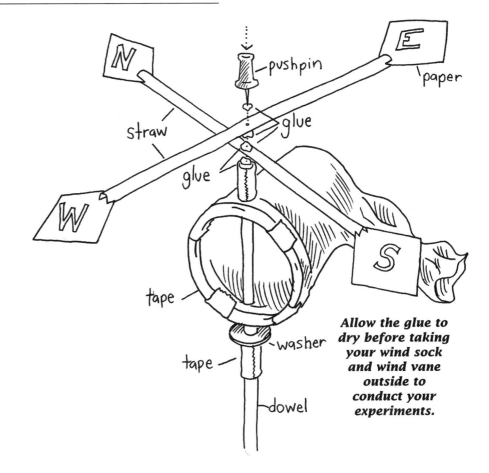

*Allow the glue to
dry before taking
your wind sock
and wind vane
outside to
conduct your
experiments.*

*Cut ¼-inch slits in each straw
end and insert 1 square of
construction paper with a
compass direction between
each pair of slits.*

2. Measure the straws and find the middle of
   each. Pierce the middle of each straw with the
   pushpin. Then dab the following surfaces with
   white glue: the top of the dowel with the pushpin hole, the middle of each straw, and the
   point of the pushpin.

3. Insert the pushpin through both straws and into the top of the dowel. Be certain the straws form a cross, with each arm 90° apart. Wipe off excess glue. Allow glue to dry before trying the experiments.

Experiments

1. Take your wind sock outside and watch it fill with wind. Wind speed increases with altitude, so use the highest (safe) location you can find to test your wind sock. Walk to the top of a nearby hill or climb to the top of the slide in a playground. If you can't find any place higher than the level ground, hold the wind sock above your head. Try to stay clear of trees and buildings. These will block the wind.

2. Use a compass to find north. Point your N straw vane in that direction. Your wind sock will turn until it faces into the wind. The wind vane will show you the direction of the wind.

   In the next activity, you can use your wind sock to determine how fast the wind is blowing.

MEASURE THE WIND WITH ADMIRAL BEAUFORT

Young Francis Beaufort joined the British Royal Navy and went to sea when he was twelve years old. For more than twenty years he learned the ways of the wind. In 1805 he devised a scale to determine the wind speed by looking at things around him—trees, flags, smoke. In later years he became Admiral Sir Francis Beaufort. Today, sailors, meteorologists, and others continue to rely on the Beaufort scale. You can find the wind speeds in your neighborhood by using your wind sock and wind vane from the previous activity and by following the Beaufort scale.

Goal *Observe and measure wind patterns at different times of the day. Calibrate (adjust) your wind sock and wind vane to the Beaufort scale.*

Materials
Beaufort scale (see page 19)

Notebook

Pencil

Wind sock and wind vane (see *Make a Wind Sock and Wind Vane* activity above)

Compass

Experiment
Take your wind sock to your backyard, school yard, or a nearby park. Find an open area, away from trees and buildings. Observe the wind in

BEAUFORT SCALE

Beaufort Number	Name of Wind	Signs/Description	Wind Speed/mph
0	calm	calm; smoke rises vertically	<1
1	light air	smoke drifts, indicating wind direction	1–3
2	light breeze	wind felt on face; leaves rustle; flags stir	4–7
3	gentle breeze	leaves and small twigs in constant motion	8–12
4	moderate breeze	small branches move; wind raises dust and loose paper	13–18
5	fresh breeze	small-leaved trees begin to sway; crested wavelets form on inland water	19–24
6	strong breeze	overhead wires whistle; umbrellas difficult to control; large branches move	25–31
7	moderate gale or near gale	whole trees sway; walking against wind is difficult	32–38
8	fresh gale or gale	twigs break off trees; moving cars veer	39–46
9	strong gale	slight structural damage occurs such as signs and antennas blown down	47–54
10	whole gale or storm	trees uprooted; considerable structural damage occurs	55–63
11	storm or violent storm	widespread damage occurs	64–74*
12	hurricane	widespread damage occurs	>74

*The United States uses 74 mph as speed criterion for a hurricane.

the same place in the morning, afternoon, and evening for five days. Watch how the wind moves different things: the tops of trees, a tall flagpole, your wind sock. Using the Beaufort scale, estimate the wind speed and record in your notebook.

Recopy the Beaufort scale in your notebook but leave room to record your own observations under the description column. Observe how your wind sock reacts to different wind speeds. Add this information to the description column on your Beaufort scale.

Find north using your compass. Point the N arm of your wind vane north. Find the wind direction using your wind sock and record in your notebook.

Results

You will probably memorize the Beaufort scale after a few days and then you'll always know how hard the wind is blowing! How could this be useful to you?

When does the wind blow strongest in your neighborhood? When is it weakest? Do you notice any wind speed pattern?

Try this experiment during different seasons. Do you see the same wind patterns in summer and winter? In the rainy season and the dry season?

What sort of geographical area do you live in—plains, valley, mountains, desert, seaside, or lakeside? How does this help to explain the wind patterns you find?

CHAPTER THREE

Windmills in Europe across the Centuries

On the windy plains of Suffolk, along the east coast of England, a strange sight appeared one day in A.D. 1191 Dean Herbert, an old priest from the local church, built a windmill with two heavy millstones to grind wheat into flour for the people of the parish.

Abbot Samson, the head of the nearby monastery, heard about the new machine and ordered his workmen to tear it down. The abbot owned the only water mill in the region. Every farmer came to his mill to grind grain into flour to make his bread, and each of them gave the abbot a share of their flour as payment. A curious mill like Herbert's windmill was bound to attract a lot of customers. This would not do.

When poor Herbert learned of the abbot's objection and realized there was no way to change his mind, Herbert ordered his own workers to take the mill apart so that, at least, he could save the lumber. The abbot's men were shocked when they arrived at the location of Herbert's mill and found nothing but the wind.

Postmills had a square box called a buck that was built around a central post and set high on a revolving platform. Large wooden sails covered with cloth faced directly into the wind. When the wind changed direction, the miller climbed down a stairway at the back, then pushed a long pole to turn the windmill. *Rijksmuseum–Stichting, Amsterdam*

The sails are attached to the cap of this smock mill. The windmiller turned only the cap when the wind changed direction. The largest, heaviest windmills were smock mills. *Rijksmuseum–Stichting, Amsterdam*

Postmills

No one knows how windmills found their way to Europe. The Crusaders, European soldiers who tried to capture Palestine from the Turks, probably saw Persian-style windmills in the Middle East. However, the windmills that appeared in Europe were nothing like the Persian ones. Perhaps they were reinvented in Europe.

These earliest European windmills are called *postmills*. These mills resemble a type of water mill found in Europe around 1200. Some historians believe that a clever person turned a water mill upside down, enlarged its paddles to catch the wind, and invented the first postmill.

Millwrights built postmills out of wood, with a few iron fastenings. The mill had to be light enough for the miller to turn, yet strong enough to withstand the fiercest storms and constant vibrations caused by spinning sails and grinding gears. The mill had to be perfectly balanced so that the millstones remained level no matter which way the mill was turned. If the stones weren't level, grain would not grind evenly. Many postmills lasted for centuries, thanks to the superb engineering skills of medieval millwrights.

Smock Mills

During the 1300s, one millwright realized that he didn't need to turn the entire postmill when the wind changed direction; he only needed to turn the sails. The sails, attached to the roof or cap of the mill, could revolve on an outdoor track. The miller turned only the cap to face the

This tall smock mill towers above the schooners docked along the Zaan River in the Netherlands.
Netherlands Board of Tourism

This small stone tower mill still runs on the Greek island of Mykonos. The cloth sails are furled, or wrapped, around the wooden arms to catch less wind. When the miller wants the sails to turn more quickly, he unfurls the sails to form large triangles that catch more wind. *Yannis Scouroyannis, Greek National Tourist Organization*

sails into the wind. The rest of the building remained fixed to the ground. This meant the mill could be bigger, heavier, and stronger. These mills reminded people of the long shirts, or smocks, that farmers wore, so they called them *smock mills.*

Windmills in Southern Europe

In the 1500s, people in Spain, Greece, and the Mediterranean islands began to build small stone windmills with triangular cloth sails. The lightweight cloth sails worked well in the lighter winds of southern Europe. In these drier countries, windmills pumped water from wells to irrigate fields and ground grain. Many old *tower windmills* still turn on the Greek island of Mykonos. The Plain of Lassithi in Crete is known as "the valley of ten thousand windmills." Today, the power of the wind is used in the same way that it was five hundred years ago.

Draining the Netherlands

"God created the world, but the Dutch created Holland" says an old Dutch proverb. The official name of the country is the Netherlands, which means low lands, for much of the country is near or below sea level. For thousands of years

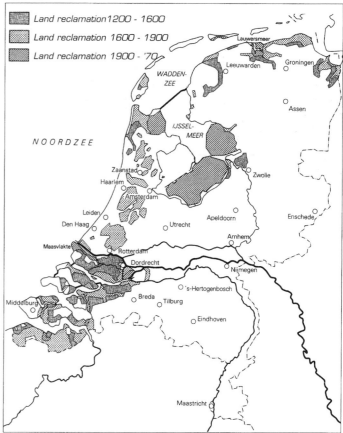

In the rainy season, these windmills at the Kinderdijk in the Netherlands pump water from the fields, through the wide canals, and out to sea. In dry times, they pump water from the large canals to the fields. The flat land in the distance, called a polder, has been reclaimed from the sea. *Royal Netherlands Embassy*

Land reclamation 1200 - 1600
Land reclamation 1600 - 1900
Land reclamation 1900 - '70

the Dutch built sea walls or dikes to hold back the sea, their fierce Waterwolf.

In the 1600s, the Dutch began to reclaim land that was below sea level. Using dikes and *drainage windmills* they pumped water out of the lakes and marshes. As the new land dried, they dug canals to channel rain water and ground water for the new farms and villages they built. These new lands were called *polders*. With the help of windmills and dikes, the Dutch were able to hold back the Waterwolf and create a country that is twice as big as before.

This map of the Netherlands shows the area below sea level that has been pumped dry since A.D. 1200 to create new land, or polders. Until the mid-nineteenth century, this work was done by windmills. Tall earthen dikes throughout the Netherlands keep back the sea. *Information and Documentation Center for the Geography of the Netherlands*

Draining the English Fens

The English also tried to drain their marshes and create new farmland. In 1588, a drainage windmill began work in the *fens* (marshes) of Lincolnshire. Adventurers with money to spend hired drainers to do the work for them. But the fiercely independent *slodgers*, who lived by hunting and fishing in the fens, liked the land as it was. As soon as the drainers would build a dike and windmill, the slodgers tore it down. Nature was on the slodgers' side, for winter storms helped to destroy the dikes and flood the land again. The battle over the fens went on for centuries. It wasn't until the mid-1800s that the drainers finally won.

Small mills, not much larger than a cow, pumped water in and out of irrigation canals in farm fields. *Seaver Center for Western History Research, Los Angeles County Museum of Natural History*

What Windmills Can Do

Windmills sprouted all over Europe and made many jobs easier and faster. By the early 1700s, the Netherlands and England each had about ten thousand windmills. Thousands more worked in France, Germany, Denmark, and Eastern Europe.

Windmills ground grain, but they also ground cocoa, gunpowder, malt, and mustard. *Paint mills* ground pigments for paint as well as herbs and chemicals to make medicines and poisons. *Oil mills* pressed the oil from seeds and millers sold the leftover seedcakes for cattle feed. *Glue mills* processed cow hides and animal bones. *Hulling mills* removed the outer layer of rice and barley kernels. *Fulling mills* pounded woolen cloth into felt. The Dutch called these stink mills because rancid butter and aged urine were used in the process. Miners used windmills to blow fresh air into deep mine shafts. Windmills also provided power to make paper and saw lumber.

Windmills came in all sizes. *Sawmills* with a crane, hoists, gears, and saws might be eighty feet tall with sails one hundred feet in diameter. Large saw frames cut giant logs, and smaller saws cut beams and boards. Leftover scraps of lumber were sent to a small twenty-five-foot windmill that cut them into strips and slats. Many farms had even smaller mills, measuring about five feet tall, to pump water from the fields.

Sawmills and paper mills grew so large—housing saws and pulp vats, storage and drying sheds—that they "split the seams" of their smock and became rectangular factories with windmills on top.

Windmill Opponents

Not everyone welcomed the new inventions. Dutch *guilds*—somewhat like our modern trade unions—protested against early industrial windmills, so the millers formed a guild of their own to promote their trade. In the 1600s, English *sawyers* who were afraid of losing their jobs, destroyed the first wind sawmill built in Deptford (near London).

In fact, windmills created new jobs. Because they drew on so much power, windmills needed many workers. In a paper mill, for example, the wind turned machines that chopped rags, churned the chopped fiber into pulp, and ground scrap paper for recycling. The whole operation needed a miller to tend the windmill and workers to tear

Windmills gave jobs to many people. Even children worked in the paper mills, tearing rags that would be made into paper. Here a woman fills a tray with pulp in a paper mill. *De Zaansche Molen, Koog aan de Zaan, Netherlands*

rags, fill the chopping and churning tubs, pour pulp into molds, hang paper up to dry, and then clean, press, and roll the paper until it was ready to be bound for shipment. Industries grew quickly when mills harnessed the wind, but all the worried English sawyers in Deptford saw was an enormous machine stronger than their own muscle power.

Building a Better Windmill

As people thought up new uses for windmills, they also thought of ways to improve them. Englishman Edmund Lee invented the *fantail* in 1745. This was a round fan of small wind vanes mounted on the back of a windmill and connected to the track that ran around the cap. When the wind changed direction, the small fantail automatically

This English windmill had a fantail on the back that automatically turned the cap when the wind changed direction. *Seaver Center for Western History Research, Los Angeles County Museum of Natural History*

swung around and moved the large sails to face directly into the wind. There would be no more dashing outside in the freezing rain or blustery gale to move the giant sails. The miller stayed inside and his fantail did the job for him. In 1759 England's John Smeaton discovered that twisting the sails about 20°, like a modern airplane propeller, gave them more power. The sails caught hold of more wind and the mills worked faster.

In 1772, Scotsman Andrew Meikle invented a wooden sail that looked like a giant shutter or Venetian blind. It was controlled by a spring set by the miller inside the mill. When the wind grew too strong, the shutters opened and slowed down the sails. England's Sir William Cubitt improved this idea by introducing a *patent sail* in 1807 that used weights and counterweights to adjust the sails smoothly and steadily. Cloth sails spun faster, but patent sails were more automatic. British millers welcomed the new inventions, but the Dutch kept their old cloth sails.

When Napoleon and the French army invaded the Netherlands in 1806, they were astonished to see hundreds of grinding, sawing, pressing, and pumping windmills along the Zaan River just north of Amsterdam. Such a concentration of industrial power existed nowhere else in the world. Wind power had created the first Industrial Revolution in Europe.

Napolean saw nearly six hundred of these windmills working on the Zaan River when he invaded the Netherlands in 1806. A few are still working. *De Zaansche Molen, Koog aan de Zaan, Netherlands*

MILL GRAIN

Dutch families used flour for pancakes, waffles, cookies, and porridge, but most of all for bread. They ate bread with each of their four meals— breakfast, dinner, mid-afternoon snack, and late-evening supper. Farm wives baked their own bread, but townsfolk bought bread from a baker. Both farm wives and bakers bought flour from the windmiller.

Goal *Grind grain by hand and experience the force needed to do the work of a windmill.*

Materials

A few handfuls of whole wheat berries (available at health food stores)

2 cement block bricks (2 by 3½ by 8 inches) *or* **1 cement block brick and a rough sidewalk**

1 tablespoon measuring spoon

Dustpan

Hand broom

Watch with second hand

Bowl

Directions

Place a handful of whole wheat berries between 2 cement bricks or on a rough sidewalk. Place 1 brick on top of the berries and grind it by applying force in a back and forth motion. Time yourself. See how long it takes to grind the berries to a flourlike consistency. Is this as fine as the whole wheat flour you buy in the store?

Sweep up the flour with a dustpan and brush. Use the tablespoon measuring spoon to see how much whole wheat flour you've ground. Count the number of tablespoons you fill as you place your whole wheat flour in a bowl.

Grind 1 brick against the bare sidewalk. Put your hand on the brick. How does it feel? What might happen in a wooden windmill if the millstones rubbed together without grain in the middle?

If a Dutch family ate one loaf of bread at every meal and each loaf uses about two cups of flour, how many cups of flour would they use each day? How long would it take you to grind this much flour with your cement block bricks? (Hint: 16 tablespoons = 1 cup)

In Chapter 4 we'll make some bread and taste how Dutch people enjoyed the results of the windmill's hard work.

WRITE ABOUT THE WIND

You can do these writing exercises alone or, with a group of people, with everyone contributing words and ideas. If you work in a group, try writing your story, legend, or journal as a play with different people acting out each role.

Goal *Use your imagination to experience the wind from different points of view and express this experience in words.*

Materials

Pen or pencil

Paper

Directions

EXERCISE 1: IMAGINE A COOL WIND ON A HOT DAY

Close your eyes and think about riding a bicycle, riding a skateboard, or roller skating on a hot, sunny day. What does the wind feel like blowing on your face? Think of words to describe this physical feeling. Open your eyes and write down your words.

Close your eyes again and get back on your imaginary bicycle, skateboard, or skates. Think of words to describe the sound of the wind. Open your eyes and write down your words. Repeat this process for seeing, tasting, and smelling the wind.

After you have compiled these lists of words describing the wind through your five senses, look at your list of words. Now write a paragraph or a poem using some of these words to describe exactly how you experienced the wind while on your bike, skateboard, or skates. (Hint: If you write a poem, try writing one that does not rhyme. You can choose from a greater variety of words this way.)

Read your paragraph or poem to someone else. Ask the person if he or she could feel the sensations about which you wrote.

EXERCISE 2: IMAGINE A COLD WIND IN A RAINSTORM

Repeat Exercise 1 while you imagine walking against a strong wind on a cold, rainy afternoon. Close your eyes and imagine each of the following senses, one at a time: sound, touch, sight, taste, and smell. Write down your descriptive words for each sense. Choose the words that best describe walking through the cold, windy rainstorm, and write a paragraph or poem about it. (Hint: Again, if you write a poem, try writing one that does not rhyme, so that you can choose from a greater variety of words.)

Read your paragraph or poem to someone else. Ask the person if he or she could feel the sensations about which you wrote.

EXERCISE 3: WRITE A STORY ABOUT THE WIND

Think of a friendly sort of wind that flies kites, pushes sailboats and windsurfers, makes waves on the water, pollinates plants, moves clouds across the sky, turns windmill sails, or makes the trees sway. Close your eyes and pretend you are a bird, a kite, a windmiller, a sailor, or a child lying on your back on the grass. A gentle wind is moving some of the things that surround you.

After a few minutes, open your eyes and begin writing a story by describing who you are, what you are doing, and what you see, hear, smell, taste, and touch. Remember that you are inventing a story, not just writing a list of words.

Now imagine that the wind is growing stronger and stronger until it turns into a storm, a hurricane, or a tornado. Perhaps it starts raining or snowing or a raging wind sweeps a fire toward you. Think about what you might see, hear, smell, taste, or touch. (Remember, you are still a bird, sailor, child, or whatever you originally imagined.)

Write about what is happening around you now. You might use parts of a true experience or you might make up the whole story.

Now imagine that the wind finally dies down. What has happened to you? What has happened to the world around you? Write a conclusion to your story.

Read your story to another person. Ask the person if he or she could feel some of the same things that you wrote about in your story.

EXERCISE 4: WRITE A LEGEND ABOUT HOW THE WIND CAME TO BE

Many cultures have legends about how the earth was made or how the first people were created. Think up a legend about how the wind came to be. Perhaps it resulted from an argument between the moon and the sun or the earth and the ocean. Perhaps the wind was the child of an unusual mother and father. Use your imagination and make your legend as fantastic as you like. Begin your story this way: *A long time ago, before there were any books or storytellers, or any humans at all, there was no wind. Then one day. . . .*

Read your legend to someone else and use different voices and movements to tell your story, like a traditional storyteller would do.

EXERCISE 5: RECORD A DAY IN THE LIFE OF THE WIND

Pretend *you* are the wind. Write a journal about a day in your life. You might make it funny or serious or both. Begin writing about this day as if it is an hour before sunrise. Where are you? Are you asleep or have you been traveling in disguise all night?

Write down your activities all through the day. Where do you go? What and who do you see? What do you do? Still pretending to be the wind, allow yourself to talk to the trees, the mountains, the ocean, or the people you meet. Record these encounters. Do you ever take a rest? Do you become angry, sad, or happy?

What happens if you do?

Continue your journal into the evening of your day and through the night, finally ending 24 hours after you started.

Read your journal to someone else using sound effects, different voices, and body movements to make your story dramatic.

Take your imagination with you next time you're outside on a windy day. See how you can experience the wind from a different point of view.

CHAPTER FOUR

A Windmiller's Life

A windmiller's life was hard but never boring. Windmillers went to work when the wind began to blow—pumping, grinding, or sawing. During heavy weather, a miller worked for days without stopping. Like a ship's captain, he remained at his post until the storm cleared, making sure his mill made it through safely. Some mills had a shaving bench where a barber shaved the miller when he was too busy to visit the barbershop.

In the late 1500s, Dutch millers had to pay a fine to the village council if they worked on Sunday. However, some of them preferred to pay the fine rather than lose a good wind. A minister once scolded a miller for working on the Lord's day. The miller replied, "If the Lord is good enough to send me wind on a Sunday, I'm going to use it!"

One windmiller might work a small water mill, but several men and their sons often worked in a grinding mill, an oil-pressing mill, a sawmill, or a paper mill. *De Zaansche Molen, Koog aan de Zaan, Netherlands*

At Home in a Windmill

A miller and his family often lived next door to a grinding mill. They often lived inside a drainage windmill that regulated water in the canals. Two doors stood on opposite sides of the mill so when the sails were blocking one door, the family could leave the mill by the other. The living room and kitchen were on the bottom floor with bedrooms up above. The miller's children swam and fished in the canals outside.

Drainage mills, often located far from town near the dikes, also served as inns for passing travelers. The miller's family was happy to have the company, and the visitor could fall asleep to the whoosh of giant windmill sails, creaking wooden gears, and splashing water.

What did windmillers look like? One old joke claimed that windmillers were short, strong, and agile—short because while others were growing, millers were busy working; strong from the heavy sacks they carried on their backs; and agile from running up and down stairs all day long to keep the windmill going.

Stormy Weather Woes

The wind often blew on sunny days, but it always blew on stormy ones. Windmillers had to go outside in all weather to turn the mill or adjust the sails. First, they rotated the *turn wheel* in the back of the mill until two sails were vertical. Then they fastened the turn wheel, put on the brake, and ran to the front of the mill. Next, they climbed about twenty feet up the wooden sail, untied the ropes that held the cloth, unfurled it,

This drainage mill housed a windmiller's family as well as the machinery to drain water from the canals. The windmiller's wife even hung curtains in the window. *Seaver Center for Western History Research, Los Angeles County Museum of Natural History*

climbed down, and tied it at the bottom of the sails. Finally they ran around the back of the mill, unfastened the turn wheel, and rotated the sails 90°. They repeated this operation four times until all the cloth sails were spread.

When the wind blew too hard, millers went outside again and *reefed* each sail. This meant rolling up the sail partway so that some wind would blow through the sail and turn it more slowly. Millers often had to adjust the reef points several times during a storm—each time stopping and starting the mill and working on one sail at a time. In winter the sails froze as hard as boards, and so did the miller's fingers and toes.

Hazards in the Mill

Millers faced many dangers. In grinding mills, millstones had to be covered with grain while the sails turned. If the

In wintertime the Dutch loved to skate on the frozen canals as shown in this photograph from 1911. They held long races that went through many villages. Skaters stopped at each windmill along the way to get their race card stamped. Those who completed the race before sunset received a medal. Today such races are held rarely because canal ice seldom freezes thick enough due to a warmer climate. *De Zaansche Molen, Koog aan de Zaan, Netherlands*

grain ran out, the stones ground against each other and created sparks– a real fire hazard. Countless wooden mills burnt to the ground even during rainstorms.

Millers sometimes sported with danger. During a storm they often kept their sails flying past the limits of safety, as each miller tried to prove himself braver than the rest. But as soon as one miller removed his sails, the other millers followed suit.

Lightning bolts, attracted to tall objects in the landscape, struck many a windmill. If lightning didn't burn the mill, its heat could fuse the metal parts in the mill's machinery, and its force could fling about everything inside the mill including the miller.

Countless millers were injured or killed by their mills. Limbs were broken and bodies were crushed by the sails or heavy gears that broke or ran out of control. A sudden *squall* could dislodge the cap of a tower mill. The wind blowing against a postmill could topple the entire structure.

Narrow escapes were common, too. For example, an English millwright named John Bryant was repairing a sail one day when the wind began to blow and the sails began to turn. The owner of the mill had neglected to fasten the brake and retired to a local tavern. To save himself from a nasty fall, Bryant jammed his hands and one leg into a wooden arm of the windmill when it began to revolve. A passerby saw what was happening and ran to put on the brake. However, when the mill came to a stop, Bryant was hanging upside down. Following Bryant's breathless instructions, the passerby helped Bryant get his feet back on the ground. But his hands were so sore that he had to attach the reins of his horse to his elbows for the carriage ride home.

Dutch families ate bread with every meal, and even the children knew how windmills helped bring fresh bread to their table. An old English nursery rhyme tells the story.

Blow, wind, blow! And go, mill, go!
That the miller may grind his corn,
That the baker may take it,
And into bread make it,
And send us some hot in the morn.

Nursery Rhymes of England by James Orchard Halliwell. Seaver Center for Western History Research, Los Angeles County Museum of Natural History

Health Hazards

Accidents weren't the only hazards of milling. The constant pounding of heavy wooden hammers against the oil press made miller's deafness common among oil millers.

A paint miller, who ground wood for paint dyes, wore a wet sponge over his mouth and nose and had to drink huge quantities of milk to keep from being poisoned by the wood dust. A miller breathed dust all day long, but milk helped "bind" the dust and remove it from his stomach before it was absorbed into his bloodstream.

When the Wind Died Down

When the wind stopped, windmillers still kept busy. Millwrights supervised major repairs, but the miller did many small repairs himself. He lubricated all the gears, including hundreds of wooden teeth, using beeswax three or four times a year. If he had any iron or steel parts he greased those with pig's fat–the older the better. Lumps of fat were hung from the rafters for twenty years or more before the miller used them to grease the metal.

A grain miller could tell if his millstones were in good condition by the color of the flour and the condition of the bran. He took a pinch of flour and rubbed it between his finger and his thumb. If it was fine enough, he gave it to the customer. If not, he hoisted it to the top of the mill and

These windmillers are grinding pigments for paint in this restored mill. The huge grindstones and giant beams and gears, along with flammable materials and toxic chemicals, made windmills a hazardous place to work. *De Zaansche Molen, Koog aan de Zaan, Netherlands*

ground it again. This was the miller's "rule of thumb" that everyone trusted. Today we still use the expression "rule of thumb" to mean a certain way of doing things that is not precisely measured or explained but that seems to work well enough for people to accept. If the flour looked a bit coarse or burned, the miller "put his nose to the grindstone" and inspected the stones. Today we use this expression when we describe someone who concentrates and works hard.

Dressing Millstones

Millstones had to be "dressed" or sharpened just right to grind the grain evenly. *Cracks* were lines cut across the millstones. When the edges of the cracks were no longer sharp, it was time to dress the millstones—usually every week or two. *Stone dressers* roamed the countryside looking for work, but some millers preferred to do the job themselves. Like many of the miller's tasks, it was an exacting one.

A grinding stone was very hard, and as a stone dresser chipped away at it, slivers of steel flew off the dressing tool and embedded themselves in the back of his hand. When an unknown stone dresser arrived in town looking for work, a miller would ask him to "show his metal." The stranger held out the back of his hand and the more blackened bits of metal the miller saw there, he assumed, the longer the man had worked at his trade. Today the expression "show your metal" means almost the same thing—show me what you've done.

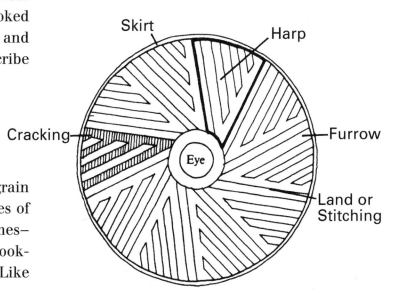

Millstones were cut or "dressed" with iron chisels so that they would grind smoothly and evenly. "Furrows" are the raised areas of the stone; "lands" are the spaces inbetween. "Cracking" are the shallow lines carved into the furrows. Some millstones were made of one large piece of stone that might weigh more than two tons. Others had eight to twenty-eight smaller stones cemented together and bound with an iron hoop or "skirt." This millstone had ten pieces shaped like harps.
John Freeman, Perth and Kinross Council, Scotland

Windmill Weatherman

The windmiller often became the village weatherman. He could tell better than anyone else when the weather would change, where the storms would break, and of course, how much the wind would blow.

Grain mills became popular gathering places in the village. Housewives visited often to buy their flour. What better place to hear the latest gossip and add a story or two of their own? The fresh tales from the windmiller often were passed around the supper table quicker than the fresh bread made from the flour he ground that day.

What's in a Name?

The Dutch grew so fond of their windmills that they passed a law in 1693 ordering that each windmill be given a name. Many had animal names: the Cat, the Seagull, the Iron Hog. Others were more sentimental: the Prince's Garden, the Darling, the Wheel of Adventure. Some were religious, perhaps to convince customers that the miller was honest: Wise Young Abraham or the Hero Joshua. A few names were downright morbid. One called Bleak Death carried a sign with a skeleton sitting on a millstone that read: "I am the end of life. Everyone should work hard to prepare for me, because I work all the time."

People invented many tales that poked fun at millers. One illustrated here was seen in old manuscripts and printed books all over Europe.

It had been a long day and the miller's horse was tired from carrying a heavy sack of grain.

"Good boy," said the miller. "You've done a hard day's work. I'll take that heavy sack off your back and carry it myself."

So the miller lifted the sack off the horse and threw it across his shoulders. After they had gone a few steps, the miller noticed the horse walking more quickly.

"Since you're not carrying the load of grain, then you can carry me," he said to the horse. So the miller put himself and the sack on the poor horse's back and made his way home.

Library of Congress, Prints and Photographs USZ62-26693

Not every miller felt so grim about his work. Two mills called De Juffer (The Young Lady) and De Jonker (The Squire) stood side by side on the Zaan River. It wasn't long before the nearby millers made up the following rhyme:

De Juffer en De Jonker
Zoenen elkaar in 't donker.

In English it goes like this:

The Young Lady and the Squire
Kissed each other in the dark.

One paper mill carried the following sign:

Rags make paper,
Paper makes money,
Money makes banks,
Banks make loans,
Loans make beggars,
Beggars make rags.
(SOURCE: MOLENMUSEUM, KOOG A/D ZAAN, NETHERLANDS)

A sense of humor sometimes made a miller's job a little easier.

"Talking" Windmills

Millers used windmills to send messages to their neighbors. When their workday was over, windmillers set their sails to form a cross. Everyone in town knew that this meant the miller had finished work for the day and would start again tomorrow morning. If the sails were set in an X,

Windmillers still decorate windmills at holiday time. The red, white, and blue–striped flag of the Netherlands flies from the top of the windmill sails. *Netherlands Board of Tourism*

"Alphonse Daudet's Windmill in Fontvieille," is a painting by Vincent van Gogh (1852–1890) who grew up in the Dutch countryside. After moving to France, he painted the windmills that reminded him of his homeland. *Amsterdam, Van Gogh Museum (Vincent Van Gogh Foundation)*

it meant the mill was closed for the weekend or the miller was on vacation. Villagers postponed a visit to the mill when the sails were set in a cross and the top sail was covered with cloth. This meant the miller was making repairs.

When his children got married or a baby was born, a miller might weave streamers through the sails and fly flags from the top sail. Other millers decorated their sails too, and turned them to face their lucky neighbor. When the top sail pointed to eleven o'clock, this meant that the miller was mourning a death in the family.

Some British millers near the seacoast hid smuggled goods in their windmills. Using sail signals, millers told smugglers to keep away when customs agents were in the neighborhood.

Some windmillers tried to protect people from danger by using sail signals. During the Protestant Reformation in the 1600s, Dutch Catholics were not allowed to practice their faith. Some windmillers positioned their sails to indicate where secret Catholic services were held each week. In 1939 when the German Army conquered the Netherlands in five days, windmills throughout the land carried the message of the invasion using the position of their sails. This gave people a few precious hours to escape or hide their valuable possessions.

During World War II, the Dutch Resistance, who fought the Germans in secret, sent windmill signals to each other. For example, when British and American pilots were shot down over the Netherlands, local windmillers signaled the airmen's location and many pilots were rescued.

Windmills began as machines to ease the hard labor of peasants. As time passed windmills and millers acquired a unique language, art, and folklore. For nearly seven hundred years windmills were the most powerful machines in Europe, well integrated into many communities. Then, during the 1800s steam engines took their place and the old windmills began to disappear from the landscape.

CREATE LANDSCAPE ART

The seventeenth century is referred to as the golden age of Dutch windmills and Dutch landscape painting. Artists painted the land around them and this land included windmills. Sometimes artists focused on the windmill alone (see Rembrandt's engraving on page 46). Other times painters gave a wide view of the land (see Ruisdael's painting on page 4 and van Gogh's painting on page 44).

Landscape painting crossed the Atlantic when Europeans settled in the New World. North America, with its vast mountains, rivers, deserts, and seacoast attracted many landscape painters in the 1800s. Today many artists still love to paint the world they see around them.

Goal *Observe and draw the world around you—draw your landscape.*

Materials
Pad of drawing paper
Pencil
Eraser
Watercolor paints, colored pencils, or crayons

Directions

Look closely at the landscape where you live. Are there hills or mountains, plains or seacoast, woods or desert? If you live in a town or city, do you have old or new buildings, high apartment houses or single-family homes, factories or office buildings? What sort of landscape lies outside the city?

Look at your landscape with an artist's eye. What would you like to draw—the view from the top of a hill or a shady spot in the park? Perhaps you prefer a busy street with shops, people, and cars going by. These views are called cityscapes.

Choose a location where you can sit for a while and make several drawings. Pencils or crayons are easiest to use when you're outside. When you're finished with a drawing, examine it. Does one thing in your scene stand out—a tree, a grain elevator, a tall building? You can draw this object up close so it appears large in the drawing or you can draw it from far away so that it blends into the landscape. Try drawing the same scene from different points of view or choose different details to emphasize.

Many artists use such drawings as guides to make larger paintings. Try making a painting of one of your sketches. Draw and paint your

landscape in different seasons. Which season do you prefer to draw?

Bonus step: Visit a local art museum or library. Look for paintings or a book of paintings that artists have made of landscapes like yours. Did they see the landscape the same way you did? Look for ideas you can use to make more landscape art.

Rembrandt van Rijn (1609–1669), one of the Netherlands' greatest artists, was the son of a windmiller. He grew up across the street from his father's malt mill in Leyden. The mill stood on the banks of the Rhine River (spelled "Rijn" in Dutch). The family took this name for their own. Here Rembrandt portrays a smock mill and the miller's house next door. *Rijksmuseum–Stichting, Amsterdam*

BAKE WHOLE WHEAT ROLLS

Traditional meals in the Netherlands always included bread. Polders (the reclaimed lands) were ideal for dairy farming, so the Dutch ate a lot of butter and cheese, too. And they still do!

Making bread takes some time (about four hours), but it's not a lot of work—most of the time the bread is rising on its own. Be sure to use a timer. If the bread rises too long or not long enough, it won't be light and tasty.

Goal *Bake and enjoy a Dutch treat.*

Ingredients

1 package dry yeast
½ cup warm water
2 cups unbleached flour
3 cups whole wheat flour
2 tablespoons honey
1½ cups warm water
4 tablespoons oil
1 teaspoon salt
1 cup whole wheat flour (for kneading)
Butter
Dutch cheese—Edam or Gouda cheese, available in your supermarket (Note: Gouda is pronounced "how-da" in Dutch.)
Apple cider

Utensils

1 medium-sized mixing bowl
1 large mixing bowl
Measuring cup
Measuring spoons
Wire whisk or wooden spoon
2 clean dish towels

(Adult help suggested.)

Stir dry yeast into ½ cup warm water. The water should be warm, but not hot (about 90° F). Let this sit for about 10 minutes, until a foam appears on top.

In the medium-sized mixing bowl, combine 2 cups unbleached flour with 3 cups whole wheat flour.

In the large bowl, mix honey, 1½ cups warm water, and oil. Stir until honey is dissolved.

Add yeast mixture and 2 cups of the flour mixture to the liquid mixture. Stir with a spoon or a whisk until all the lumps are gone. This will be a soupy mixture similar to pancake batter. It's called a sponge.

Use a clean dish towel to cover the bowl containing your sponge and set it in a warm place (between 70° and 80° F). Don't set in a drafty place. If your stove has pilot lights you can put it on top of an (unlighted) burner or in the unheated oven. Let it rise until it doubles in size—about 1 hour.

Add the salt to the rest of the flour. Add this mixture to the bowl containing the sponge. Stir until thoroughly mixed. You will have a sticky dough.

Sprinkle some whole wheat flour on a clean, dry counter and on your hands. Remove the sticky sponge dough from the bowl. Knead the dough by pressing it into the counter with the heels of your hands. Do this 2 or 3 times, then fold the dough in half and add more flour to the counter and your hands. Continue to knead for about 10 minutes, until the dough is smooth, elastic, and no longer sticky. (Note: You may use less than 1 cup of flour while kneading, or you may use a bit more.)

Return the dough to a clean large mixing bowl, cover with a towel and set in a warm place to rise until it doubles in size, 45–60 minutes.

When the dough has risen, punch it down to its original size and shape into small balls about 2 inches in diameter. Place these spread out in 2 well-oiled round cake pans. (They will expand and join together while they cook.) Cover the rolls with dish towels and let rise another 20 minutes.

Preheat oven to 375° F. Bake rolls for 20–25 minutes or until golden brown.

Yield: 24 rolls

Eat your Dutch rolls hot from the oven. Spread them with butter or Dutch cheese or both. Apple cider is a favorite drink in Holland. Try it with your Dutch treat!

CHAPTER FIVE

All-American Windmills

"*Goede morgen, Mevrouw Pietersen,*" said the miller to the plump Dutch housewife entering his windmill.

"*Ook goede morgen, Mijnheer de Molenaar,*" she said to the miller as a screech filled the air.

"*The sawmill received a shipment this morning,*" explained the miller. "*That's the first log going through the saw. This strong wind may last for two or three days, and you can be sure the sawyers will keep us awake tonight.*"

Where was this scene? It could have been in many Dutch towns in the 1600s, but it was actually thousands of miles away in New York City. Dutch merchants bought the island of Manhattan in 1626, named it New Amsterdam, and began to settle there. They didn't keep it for long. In 1664 the English took over and changed the name to New York. By that time, the Dutch had built a string of windmills from the Battery to Park Row. When the government changed hands, most Dutch settlers stayed in New York and so did their windmills.

The Dutch bought the island of Manhattan from the Indians in 1626 and called their settlement New Amsterdam. Windmills were a common sight along the Hudson River. When the English took over in 1664 the windmills remained. *Seaver Center for Western History Research, Los Angeles County Museum of Natural History*

This early windmill was built on top of a hill in Newport, Rhode Island, to catch the breeze that blows off the water. Rhode Island, Cape Cod, and Long Island have many old windmills restored to working order. *Library of Congress, Prints and Photographs, USZ62-32567*

Windmills were so important in colonial New York City that the official city seal, designed in 1784, shows four windmill sails and two barrels of flour. This seal is still used today. *New York City Department of General Services*

Dutch millwrights also built windmills in Breukelen (Brooklyn) and up the Hudson River Valley. English millwrights built smock mills and postmills from Cape Cod to Long Island and south to the Carolinas. Windmillers worked their windmills just as they had done in Europe.

Inventors Take Up the Challenge

Until 1850, the American West belonged to Native North Americans who followed herds of bison and made camp near rivers and streams. When white settlers first looked west, across the Mississippi River, they saw land that was too dry to farm or graze cattle on. They even nicknamed it the Great American Desert. There didn't seem to be enough water to make this region habitable.

In 1860, a Texan wrote to *Scientific American* magazine "The great want of Texas is water. . . . There is a million dollars lying waiting for the first man who will bring us a windmill–strong, durable, and controllable." Dozens of inventors took up the challenge.

In Connecticut, a mechanic named Daniel Halladay claimed he could invent a windmill that would automatically stop working in high winds. But he couldn't imagine "a single man in the world who would want one." John Burnham knew otherwise. He fixed windmills that broke because farmers were too busy to take down the sails when the wind blew too hard. He persuaded Halladay to put his Yankee ingenuity to work.

Halladay invented a small windmill on a wooden tower. Gone was the smock that held it up and gone were the four huge sails that caught the wind. Instead, Halladay arranged a dozen or more thin wooden slats around a hub. When the wind blew too hard, the fan of wind vanes swung so the wind blew through them and saved the mill from blowing apart.

Halladay didn't have much success selling his windmills in New England, so he and Burnham moved to Chicago–the Windy City. They set up a windmill factory in nearby Batavia, Illinois.

Reverend Leonard R. Wheeler, who ran a Christian mission for Native North Americans in Wisconsin, also invented a new windmill. Like Halladay, he used a simple tower and thin wooden wind vanes, but

An ad from the 1870s shows the many tasks that windmills performed on the farm, at the railroad depot, and at an elegant country villa. *Library of Congress, Prints and Photographs USZ 62-13210*

Nineteenth-century factory-made windmills were small, easily assembled, and relatively cheap. They used interchangeable parts, ran automatically, and needed little care. Many American farms and ranches were so large that a rancher might not visit his windmill for months. *Original advertising card, Batavia Historical Society, Batavia, Illinois*

his machine had a small side wind vane that turned the whole wheel sideways in a strong wind. He called it the Eclipse.

The new American windmills were less powerful than the old European models, but they could do the job that was needed–pumping water. Strictly speaking, they weren't windmills because they didn't mill (grind); they pumped. But everyone called them windmills nonetheless.

Windmills on the Railroad

After the Civil War ended in 1865, people rushed to settle the West. Railroads snaked their way across the Great Plains. These coal-burning steam locomotives needed about two thousand gallons of water every twenty miles. Railroad workers collected water from streams, railroad cars filled with water, and windmills.

The railroad trade was a prize for any windmill company. Union Pacific bought seventy giant *Halladay windmills* for the first transcontinental railroad. Smaller Eclipse mills watered the engines of the Burlington, Northwestern, Illinois Central, and Atchison, Topeka, and Santa Fe railroads. Large windmills could lift water 150 feet. They began to turn at wind speeds as low as six mph.

The steam locomotives that crossed the American prairies used about two thousand gallons of water every twenty miles. This station at Laramie, Wyoming, was far from any river, so a giant windmill pumped water from deep underground. *American Heritage Center, University of Wyoming*

Windmills on the Farm

Some farmers couldn't afford a factory-built windmill, so they made their own. This eight-bladed Battle-Ax windmill photographed in 1898 near Grand Island, Nebraska, cost $14 to make. *U.S. Geological Survey Photographic Library, Barbour Collection #21*

Farmers needed water for their houses and vegetable gardens, and ranchers had to fill livestock watering troughs. Pioneers bought windmills and towers from traveling salesmen or from mail-order catalogs. Some people saved money by building the towers themselves. Most companies painted the company's name on the *rudder*, but Sears Roebuck offered to paint the owner's name free of charge.

Many farmers had no money to spare, so they built their own windmills. In 1897, Professor Erwin Barbour of the University of Nebraska sent students on a field trip to photograph these homemade windmills. They left Lincoln, Nebraska, with horses, camping wagons, and cameras and traveled to Denver, Colorado. The students found wind machines made from bits of broken machinery, scrap iron, and wood. These mills had nicknames like Go-Devil, Ground Tumbler, Jumbo, Baby Jumbo, Merry-Go-Round, and Battle-Ax. They weren't as efficient as factory models, but that didn't seem to matter. Professor Barbour said, "they cost little, work well, and do all the work that is laid on them."

The Great Plains suffered terrible droughts that could last for years. Windmills couldn't irrigate the vast fields of wheat and corn that the farmers grew as cash crops, but they could water an acre of vegetables near the farmhouse. In drought years, a windmill could mean the difference between survival and starvation.

A child in Cherry County, Nebraska said it in poetry.

We like it in the sandhills,

We like it very good,

For the wind it pumps our water,

And the cows they chop our wood.

(How did cows chop wood? They didn't really. The Western plains had few, if any, trees to chop. Instead pioneers burned buffalo or cow chips—manure that had dried in the hot prairie sun. It wasn't really wood and cows didn't chop it, but cows did provide fuel to cook the meals and heat the sod houses of early settlers. And out in the yard the wind pumped all the water they needed.)

These Nebraska homesteaders from the 1880s made their sod house by hand but bought a factory-made windmill. The family probably owned little more than what we see here—a few horses, some cattle, and a windmill. *Nebraska State Historical Society*

Hardy Workers

Windmills performed many labor-saving tasks in the American West. They sawed wood and ran the cotton gin. They hoisted grain into tall silos. They pumped water from mine shafts and crushed ore when it came out of the ground. They ran turning lathes for carpenters and even powered a printing press in Sauk Center, Minnesota. The newspaper editor couldn't resist a joke about his windmill press. He said "wind is an important agent in the running of political newpapers, especially about election time, but its employment in such prosaic service as doing useful commercial printing is, we believe, quite exceptional."

One proud owner bragged that his Eclipse windmill "grinds all the feed for six horses and twenty-four head of cattle and hogs, shells all the corn, does all the pumping for the stock, saws all our wood, and runs a wooden-turn lathe and grindstone. It does all the churning every day, runs a washing machine, and last but not least, runs a crank pipe organ so that the girls can have a song and dance while the machine is doing their work. This may sound a little strange, but it is perfectly true."

Strange? Yes. True? Perhaps.

Gold miners in California needed salt to preserve their meat and process ore, so enterprising men built salt works in San Francisco Bay. This 1912 photograph shows how windmills pumped saltwater from one evaporation pond to another. *U.S. Geological Survey Photographic Library, Phalen Collection #329*

CREATE A WINDMILL PAPER COLLAGE

Early American settlers made almost everything they needed. Women sewed clothing for the family. They used pieces of leftover fabric and worn-out clothes to make patchwork quilts. Quilt making gave women a chance to express artistic ideas in a practical way. They took objects from daily life—like wedding rings, log cabins, and windmills—and invented quilt patterns that reminded them of those objects.

Goal *Create a windmill pattern out of colorful paper.*

Materials

1 sheet of heavy drawing paper or poster board, 8½ by 11 inches

3 pieces of construction paper or gift wrap of different colors or patterns

Color 1: 3½ by 7 inches

Color 2: 3½ by 3½ inches

Color 3: 3½ by 3½ inches (This will make the windmill sails and should be brighter than the other pieces; or try a patterned paper.)

Tools

Scissors

Ruler

Pencil

Glue

Directions

1. Fold Color 1 in half to make 2 3½-inch squares. Cut on fold line. Fold these squares on the diagonal and cut along the fold. This will make 4 right-angle triangles.

2. Fold Color 2 in half to make 2 right-angle triangles, each right-angle side measuring 3½ inches. Cut along the fold.

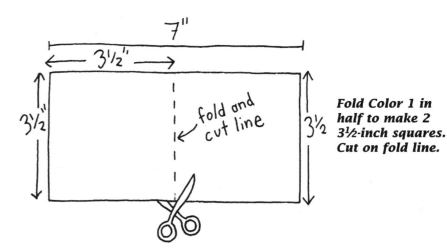

Fold Color 1 in half to make 2 3½-inch squares. Cut on fold line.

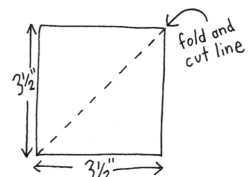

Fold Color 1 squares on the diagonal and cut. This makes 4 right triangles.

Fold Color 2 squares in half to make 2 right triangles. Cut along the fold. Do the same for Color 3. For colors 2 and 3, fold on the diagonals again and cut.

3. Fold Color 3 in half to make 2 right-angle triangles, each right-angle side measuring 3½ inches. Cut along the fold.

4. Fold Color 2 and Color 3 triangles on the diagonal again. Cut along the fold. You will have 4 small right-angle triangles, each right-angle side measuring 2½ inches.

5. Lay all the triangles on the heavy paper, using it as a picture frame, to form a windmill pattern. Be sure the windmill sails are in the right position. Leave a border on all sides. With a pencil and ruler, lightly draw along the outside edge of your collage.

6. Glue each triangle in place on the picture frame. When finished, display your collage by pinning it to a bulletin board or hanging it on a wall. Can you see the windmill sails spin?

   You can also make a collage using pieces of fabric. Instead of using glue to secure the triangles, use a needle and thread.

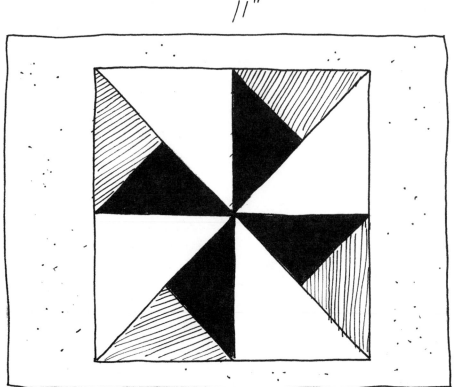

Make sure the windmill sails are facing the right direction.

SEW A WINDMILL POT HOLDER

You can sew this pot holder by hand or on a sewing machine.

Goal *Create a windmill-patterned pot holder with colorful fabric.*

Materials

4 pieces of fabric of different colors or patterns
Color 1: 3½ by 7 inches
Color 2: 3½ by 3½ inches
Color 3: 3½ by 3½ inches (This will represent the windmill sails and should be brighter than the other pieces; or try a pattern.)
Color 3: 7 by 7 inches. This will form the back of the pot holder and should match the windmill sails.
1 piece of cotton batting, 6 by 6 inches
Scissors
Straight pins
Needle and thread
Iron and ironing board
1 plastic ring, ½ inch in diameter

Directions

(Adult help suggested.)

1. Fold and cut Color 1 in half to make 2 3½-inch squares. Fold the Color 1 squares on the diagonal and cut along the fold. You will have four right-angle triangles, each right-angle side measuring 3½ inches.

2. Fold colors 2 and 3 on the diagonal and cut along the fold. You will have 4 right-angle triangles, each right-angle side measuring 3½ inches. Fold colors 2 and 3 triangles on the diagonal again. Cut along the fold. You will have 8 small right-angle triangles, each right-angle side measuring 2½ inches.

3. Lay all your triangles on a table to form the windmill pattern illustrated on page 60. Be sure your windmill sails are in the right position.

4. Pin the smaller triangles together (colors 2 and 3), with the right sides of the fabric together. You'll make 4 right-angle triangles, each right-angle side measuring 3½ inches.

5. Sew these triangles together with a ¼-inch seam. Iron the seams flat.

6. Form the windmill pattern again. Pin the sewn triangle to a Color 1 triangle to form a square. Pin the right sides of the fabric together. Repeat until you have 4 squares.

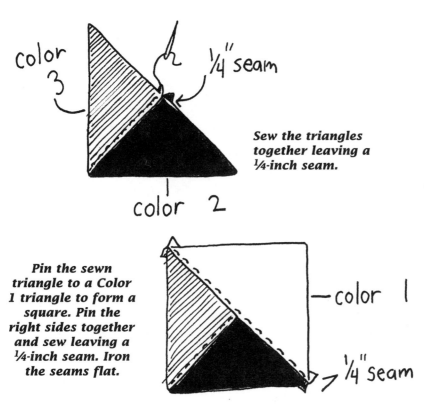

color 3

¼" seam

Sew the triangles together leaving a ¼-inch seam.

color 2

Pin the sewn triangle to a Color 1 triangle to form a square. Pin the right sides together and sew leaving a ¼-inch seam. Iron the seams flat.

—color 1

¼" seam

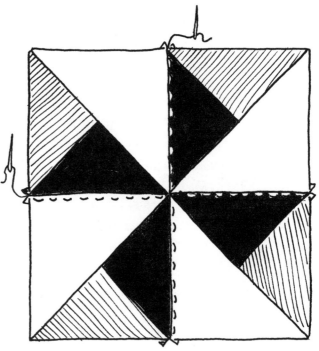

Form the windmill pattern and pin together. Sew the horizontal and vertical seams with a ¼-inch seam.

7. Sew the squares together with a ¼-inch seam. Iron the seams flat.

8. Form the windmill pattern again with your 4 squares. Pin your 4 squares together, right sides of the fabric together, to form 1 large square, approximately 6½ inches on each side. You'll have 1 6½-inch vertical seam and one 6½-inch horizontal seam.

9. Sew the seams with a ¼-inch seam. Iron the seams flat.

10. Lay the windmill pattern square on the 7 by 7-inch Color 3 square, with right sides of the fabric together. Pin 3 sides of the square. Sew the 3 sides with a ¼-inch seam.

11. Turn the pot holder right side out. Insert the square of batting.

12. Fold the 2 open edges of the square to make a seam. Pin the edges, and then sew them together. Sew the plastic ring to 1 corner of the pot holder so you can hang it up for all to see.

MAKE A WINDMILL PILLOW COVER

Make four windmill squares to cover a small cushion or pillow. Organize an old-fashioned quilting bee—invite some friends to help and you'll be surprised how fast the work gets done.

Goal *Create a windmill pattern on a decorative pillow.*

Materials

4 pieces of fabric of different colors or patterns

Color 1: 7 by 14 inches

Color 2: 7 by 7 inches

Color 3: 7 by 7 inches (This will represent the windmill sails and should be brighter than the other pieces; or try a patterned piece.)

Color 3: 13 by 13 inches (This will form the back of the pillow.)

Scissors

Straight pins

Needle and thread

Iron and ironing board

1 pillow or uncovered cushion, 12 by 12 inches

7–9 medium-sized snaps

Directions

(Adult help suggested.)

1. Fold and cut Color 1 in quarters to make 4 pieces, each 3½ by 7 inches.

2. Fold and cut colors 2 and 3 into quarters to make 4 pieces, each 3½ inches square.

3. Select 1 piece each of colors 1, 2, and 3 and set the others aside.

4. Follow windmill pot holder directions, Steps 1–9. Make 3 more windmill pattern squares (4 in all).

5. Pin the 4 squares together, right sides of the fabric together. You will have 1 12-inch vertical seam and 1 12-inch horizontal seam. Sew together with a ¼-inch seam. Iron the seams flat.

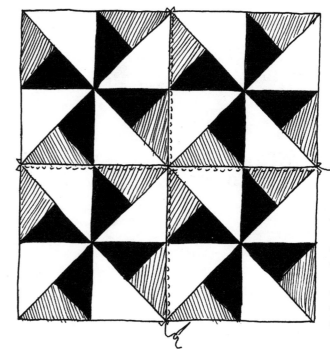

Pin 4 squares together and sew ¼-inch seam along the vertical and horizontal seams. Iron the seams flat.

6. Lay the big windmill pattern on your 13 by 13-inch square, with right sides together. Pin 3 sides of the square. Sew the 3 sides with a ¼-inch seam. Turn the pillow cover right side out.

7. Hem both raw edges on the fourth side of the square as follows. Fold the raw edge ¼ inch. Then fold another ¼ inch to make a smooth edge. Sew seam. Repeat with second raw edge. One side of the pillow cover will still be open.

8. Sew snaps every 2 inches on the 2 open ends of the pillow cover. Be sure the 2 parts of the snaps line up with each other.

9. Insert the pillow into the pillow cover and put it in a prominent place for all to see.

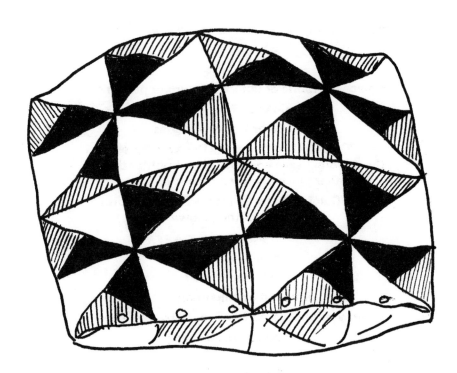

Stuff the pillow or cushion into the pillow cover.

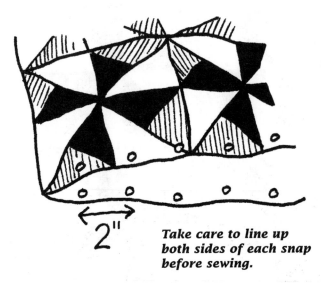

2"

Take care to line up both sides of each snap before sewing.

BAKE COLONIAL APPLE-CRANBERRY COBBLER

New England settlers brought apple cobbler from England and discovered native cranberries in North America. Cranberries alone are sour, but when mixed with apples and sugar, they form a sweet-and-sour treat. Colonial millers ground whole wheat flour, but you can mix whole wheat and white flour if you like.

Goal *Bake and enjoy a sweet New England treat.*

FRUIT

4 or 5 green cooking apples

1 cup whole cranberry sauce

3 tablespoons brown sugar

TOPPING

1 cup whole wheat pastry flour or ½ cup white flour and ½ cup whole wheat flour

1 tablespoon white sugar

1 teaspoon baking powder

½ teaspoon baking soda

¼ teaspoon salt

3 tablespoons butter

½ cup milk

Ice cream, yogurt, or milk

Utensils

Knife

Measuring cup

Casserole dish

Large mixing bowl

Measuring spoons

Pastry cutter or fork

Large spoon

Directions

(Adult help suggested.)

Preheat oven to 350° F. Slice apples to make 4 cups. Place in lightly greased casserole dish. Add cranberry sauce and brown sugar; mix thoroughly. In bowl combine flour, white sugar, baking powder, baking soda, and salt. Add butter. Using a pastry cutter or fork, cut up the butter until completely blended with flour mixture. Add milk and stir. The dough will be sticky. Drop spoonfuls of the dough on top of the fruit to make your "cobbles." A fruit cobbler is meant to look like a bumpy cobblestone street, so don't make your topping modern-highway smooth. Also, don't try to cover every bit of fruit. The dough will spread out during baking. Bake for 40 minutes or so, until the crust is golden brown.

You can use your windmill-patterned pot holder to take the Colonial Apple-Cranberry Cobbler out of the oven. Eat it while it's hot topped with ice cream, yogurt, or milk.

CHAPTER SIX

Inventors and Cowboys Work the Wind

In the early 1880s, Thomas O. Perry, an engineer at Daniel Halladay's U.S. Wind Engine and Pump Company, conducted the first scientific studies of windmills. Perry invented a wind tunnel and steam-powered sweep (wind machine) that spun windmills at controlled speeds. He also invented instruments to measure wind speeds, temperature, and barometric pressure.

Perry completed more than five thousand windmill experiments. He tested many different models in different wind and climate conditions. He tinkered with the size and shape of the wind vanes. He tried different materials. He attached wind vanes at different angles. Some people laughed at Perry's scientific principles and his mathematical windmill, but that didn't stop him.

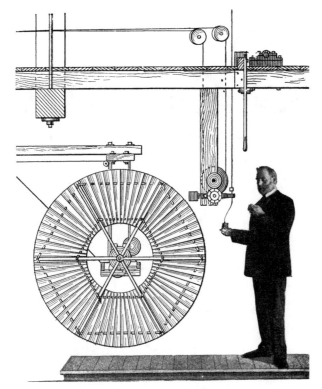

In the 1880s Thomas O. Perry performed more than five thousand experiments on windmills. This fanciful collage shows him with part of his scientific apparatus. *U.S. Geological Survey Water Supply Paper, 1899*

He wanted to design a windmill that would work in light as well as heavy winds. He replaced flat wooden blades with concave steel blades set at a new angle to produce low wind resistance and high strength. Perry worked for more than a year in a locked test chamber with guards at the door. He claimed that he locked it to control his experiments. Some people said he was afraid of spies. When he was satisfied with his results, he presented his new windmill to the board of directors at Halladay's company. They rejected it. Halladay's company, which had been so revolutionary back in the 1850s, had grown conservative in middle age. So Perry took his design elsewhere. He met inventor-businessman La Verne Noyes and together they started the Aermotor Company to manufacture Perry's *mathematical windmill.*

Wood Versus Steel

Early windmills were made of wood with a few metal fittings. Metal wind vanes were often weak and always hard to repair. They also rusted easily. Makers of wooden mills boasted that "All good wood mills will outlast two steel mills of anybody's make."

Aermotor's new design converted many owners–but not all–from wooden to steel windmills. But disagreements didn't stop there.

Metal windmill owners argued about the best way to prevent rust on the steel mills. Some favored paint; others favored galvanizing. This meant dipping the metal parts into molten zinc–an element that resists rust. In the galvanizers' camp, there were groups that believed in galvanizing windmill parts before they were put together. Others insisted on galvanizing afterward. Western ranchers and farmers were an independent lot. They never agreed on one best windmill.

A Matter of Pride

By 1889 there were seventy-seven windmill companies in the United States and intense rivalries sprang up. It was not just about who sold more windmills; it was also about loyalty. Windmill factory workers took pride in their work.

In 1893 the World's Columbian Exposition opened in Chicago, and twenty-one million people wandered through two hundred buildings to see the most advanced technology from around the world. A person would have to walk 150 miles just to see all of the latest inventions in electricity, machinery, and many other fields. Giant steam engines, Thomas Edison's talking films, and the world's largest Ferris wheel drew the biggest crowds.

Tucked in back of the agriculture hall dozens of old familiar windmills, from fifteen different companies, blew in the breeze. A smock mill, imported from the Netherlands, ground cocoa while Dutch girls in traditional costume served hot chocolate. American windmills ground and chopped cattle feed, shelled corn, pumped water, and sawed lumber.

The owners of the Aermotor Company saw a chance to attract more attention by erecting a windmill behind the livestock pavilion to cut and grind feed for the animals. Other companies protested. They wanted extra publicity, too. Harsh words flew back and forth. One evening,

Perry's windmill used concave steel blades set at a precise angle to spin faster and last longer. But some ranchers liked their old flat, wooden-bladed windmills and saw no reason to adopt the new "mathematical" model. *Panhandle-Plains Historical Museum, Research Center, Canyon, Texas*

while the Aermotor crew was at dinner, a group of men stole into the livestock area and pulled down the windmill. Tempers grew even hotter and fights broke out. Aermotor rebuilt it and offered to pay shipping charges to bring other windmills to the livestock pavilion, but by then the exposition was nearly over. In the end, only the *Aermotor windmill* rose above the pigpens.

American Windmills Abroad

American windmills traveled far afield. In 1906 a reporter named Frank O. Medlock wrote, "From the mining camps of Alaska, where it pumps water to wash out the gold, to the very heart of Africa, where it grinds grain for the natives, and so on clear around the globe, the windmill is faithfully doing its work. Windmills are exported from the United States to South America, South Africa, Australia, and other agricultural and grazing countries. But the United States is the greatest country in the world for windmills."

America still exports windmills today. The old-style American windmill is still the cheapest way to pump water in dry, windy lands.

One visitor described the Chicago Columbian Exposition windmills this way: "numerous tall towers, like the masts of ships grouped closely in harbor with colors flying, surmounted by wind wheels of various forms and sizes whirling, in the bright sunlight and throwing off sparkling rays of many colors that afford from the distance a unique, lively, and brilliant spectacle." *Illinois State Historical Library*

Windmillers of the Wild West

As windmills sprang up across the Great Plains, so did a new character—
the American windmiller. His European cousin would never have rec-
ognized him. In Europe, windmills passed from father to son, and a
family of millers often lived in the same town for centuries. They never
went far from home, worked day and night at the mill, and knew everyone in town.

Windmillers camped out as
they traveled from ranch to
ranch. A cook who could
make good beans and coffee
over a campfire was wel-
come on any crew.
*Panhandle-Plains Historical
Museum, Research Center,
Canyon, Texas*

High on the towers, millers oiled the windmills and replaced broken parts. They also repaired the pumps that lifted the water from deep underground. *Panhandle-Plains Historical Museum, Research Center, Canyon, Texas*

American windmillers were different in almost every respect. They were loners, traveling from ranch to ranch in horse-drawn wagons, each with a tool chest and perhaps a dog to keep him company. Many were former cowboys, but they didn't even sleep in the bunkhouse with the other hired hands. Nighttime found them camping in their wagons or under the stars.

Though the rancher hardly knew him, a windmiller was as important to him as the traveling doctor or the veterinarian. When a new windmill arrived from the factory, a windmiller helped the rancher put it together. He also checked, greased, and repaired old mills and water pumps. Repairing windmills could be dangerous, for a strong prairie wind could blow a man off a hundred-foot tower.

All around the Windmill Tower

Windmillers weren't the only ones to climb the windmill towers. Boys and girls often sneaked up to take a look at the finest view in the country. For example, one boy rigged up an airborne trolley by stringing a wire from the windmill tower to the house. Another group of children were spanked for climbing a windmill tower. These adventurous spirits were stopped only when their father sawed off the ladder about eight feet up.

Many grown-ups feared these heights. The huge XIT Ranch in Texas, spread over three million acres, had more than five hundred windmills. Ranch hands oiled the windmills when they needed it. But some wives offered free cooking and laundry to anyone who would take

As farmers became more prosperous, they moved from cramped sod houses to comfortable farmhouses. But rich or poor, they all needed a windmill to work the farm. *Illinois State Historical Library*

their husbands' turn at oiling the windmill. When self-oiling windmills were invented, both cowboys and their wives breathed easier.

Windmill towers proved to be useful in other ways. Farmers hung lanterns from the towers to serve as beacons for travelers. Cowboys climbed to the tops of towers to look for their cattle. Ministers sometimes baptized Christians at the windmill's water tank, and more than one outlaw was hanged from a windmill tower.

As the West grew more civilized, folks used windmills to pump water through pipes of their indoor plumbing—a sink in the kitchen and a toilet and bathtub in the bathroom. They would have no more outhouses and washtubs in the kitchen.

Six million windmills worked in the West during their heyday—1880 to 1935. "The prairie land is fairly alive with them," said the *Kansas City Star* in 1904. "The windmill has taken the place of the old town pump, and no Western town is complete in its public comforts without a mill supplying water to man and beast by the energy of the wind."

Today, some of the old windmills have been restored by historical societies and individual collectors. This Halladay windmill, with its vanes tilted to avoid damage in heavy winds, has been restored and installed by the Batavia Illinois Historical Society along a river walk. It remains a powerful symbol of the early history of the American West. For other locations of restored windmills, see "Where to Find Windmills." *Bob Popeck, Batavia, Illinois*

PRAIRIE COOKIN' CORN DODGERS

Windmillers, cowboys, and settlers on the Great Plains ate corn bread and beans almost every day—for breakfast, lunch, or supper. Corn bread took on many names from New England to California. Folks called it jonnycake, journeycake, or hoecake. If they didn't have an oven to bake it, they cooked little cakes in a skillet and called them corn dodgers. Out on the prairie, cowboys and windmillers cooked corn dodgers over a campfire.

Goal *Cook and eat a traditional prairie cowboy dish.*

Ingredients
1 cup coarse yellow cornmeal
½ teaspoon salt
1 tablespoon brown sugar
2 tablespoons oil
1 cup boiling water
1 egg
Honey or maple syrup

Utensils
Measuring cup
Measuring spoons
Large mixing bowl
Large spoon for mixing
Frying pan or griddle
Spatula

Directions
(Adult help suggested.)

Mix cornmeal, salt, and brown sugar. Add 1 tablespoon of oil and stir until blended. Add boiling water and mix thoroughly. Beat in egg. The dough will be sticky but not runny. Preheat a frying pan or griddle with 1 tablespoon of oil. To test if it's hot enough, sprinkle a few drops of water in the pan. When this water sizzles, the pan is ready. Turn heat to low. Drop spoonfuls of batter into the pan. Cook for about 5 minutes or until lightly browned. Turn and cook five minutes on the other side. Eat your crispy corn dodgers plain or pour honey or maple syrup on top for a sweet treat.

COOK ON-THE-TRAIL BEANS

Goal *Cook and sample another prairie trail dish.*

Ingredients

1 pound dry pinto beans

6 cups water

3 cloves garlic, minced

1 onion, finely chopped

1 teaspoon dried sage leaves

3 tablespoons oil

3 tablespoons imitation bacon bits

Salt to taste

Pepper to taste

Utensils

Large pot with lid

Measuring cup

Measuring spoons

Large spoon for mixing

Ladle

Potato masher

Directions

(Adult help suggested.)

Rinse the beans. Place the beans in a large pot. Add water, garlic, onion, sage leaves, and oil. Cover and let beans soak for 4 hours or overnight. When you are ready to cook the beans, remove the lid and add imitation bacon bits, and salt and pepper to taste. Bring the mixture to a boil, and then lower the heat and simmer for about 1 hour or until tender. Stir several times during cooking. Use a ladle to dish them into a soup bowl, or mash them with a potato masher and serve on a plate.

Call your friends and family to the table with the traditional "Cowboy's Gettin'-Up Holler." Windmillers, just like cowboys, traveled from one ranch to another. They probably heard this call every morning.

COWBOY'S GETTIN'-UP HOLLER

Wake up Jacob Day's a breakin'
Fryin' pan's on and hoecakes bakin'.
Beans are in the pan and coffee's in the pot,
Get up now and get it while it's hot.

SING A SONG OF THE AMERICAN WEST

In 1862 Congress passed the Homestead Act, which gave 160 acres of land *free* to unmarried adults or heads of households. In order to gain title to (ownership of) the land, homesteaders needed to build a house on their land claim and live in it for five years. People didn't need money to obtain their government claim, but they did need a strong constitution *and* a sense of humor. The same wind that powered the windmills to pump water also brought blizzards, dust storms, tornadoes, and prairie fires that tested their resolve.

Goal *Learn about the hardships of early pioneers in song.*

After supper, serenade your family or friends with this traditional folk song about pioneer life in the old West. If someone you know plays harmonica, ask him or her to accompany you—it'll lend an authentic cowboy sound to your song. (The melody and guitar cords follow.)

STARVING TO DEATH ON MY GOVERNMENT CLAIM

Tom White is my name, an old bachelor I am,
You'll find me out West in the country of fame,
You'll find me out West on an elegant plain,
And starving to death on my government claim.

Hurrah for Nebraska! the land of the free,
The land of the bedbug, grasshopper, and flea,
I'll sing of its praises and tell of its fame,
While starving to death on my government claim.

My house is built of natural sod,
Its walls are erected according to hod;
Its roof has no pitch but is level and plain,
I always get wet if it happens to rain.

How happy am I when I crawl into bed!
A rattlesnake hisses a tune at my head,
A gay little centipede, all without fear,
Crawls over my pillow and into my ear.

Good-bye to Nebraska where blizzards arise,
Where the sun never sinks and a flea never dies,
And the wind never ceases but always remains
Till it starves us all out on our government claims.

Farewell to Nebraska, farewell to the West,
I'll travel back East to the girl I love best,
I'll go to Kentucky and marry me a wife,
And quit corn bread and beans for the rest of my life.

CHAPTER SEVEN

A New Kind of Windmill

In 1892, while windmills watered the American Great Plains, inventor Poul LaCour worked on a new sort of windmill in his native Denmark. Denmark is a flat country where the wind blows more than three hundred days a year. Thousands of Dutch-style windmills already ground grain for flour and cattle feed, but LaCour's dream was to work the wind in a new way. In 1892 he succeeded in generating electricity with an old-fashioned Dutch windmill.

LaCour took his invention to the Danish government and in 1903 the Danish Wind Electricity Company was formed. Within five years, seventy-two wind-powered generators were providing electricity to farms and villages.

In 1894, Norwegian explorer Fridtjof Nansen sailed the Arctic Ocean searching for the exact location of the North Pole. During the long dark winter, his ship was trapped in the Arctic ice. The sun never rose above the horizon for months at a time, but Nansen's cabin glowed with electric lights thanks to LaCour's invention. Nansen had taken a small windmill and generator with him. While the great cities of New York and Paris were lit by gaslight, one small ship at the North Pole shone bright with wind-powered electric lights.

In 1892 Danish inventor Poul LaCour invented a windmill that generated electricity. He used a Dutch-style mill with large wooden sails. By 1908 Denmark had seventy-two windmills providing low-cost electricity to farms and villages. *Askov Højskole, Vejen, Denmark*

Windmills Bring Radio to the Farm

During the 1920s a new invention–radio–captivated American families. But radios required electricity and most farms had none. But most farms did have windmills. Some farmers tried generating electricity with their water pumping mills, but these didn't spin fast enough. So they tried another new invention that twirled–an airplane propeller.

Farmyard tinkers went to work using automobile generators, a storage battery, and airplane or hand-carved propellers. Many barns were crowned by these electric windmills that ran the radio and lit a few lightbulbs besides. Homemade generators could produce three hundred to six hundred watts of electricity.

Soon, more ambitious inventors improved these designs. Marcellus Jacobs, who grew up on a windy ranch in Montana, worked for years on his wind machine. He tried metal blades but decided wood was better. He settled on three blades for his propeller and invented a new kind of generator. In 1937, Jacobs and his brother opened the Jacobs Wind Electric Company in Minneapolis, Minnesota, and over the years sold tens of thousands of small generating windmills all over the world.

The *Jacobs windmill* could produce four hundred to five hundred *kilowatt-hours* per month in a windy location. This could run lights, radios, or power tools in the barn. Like the oldest windmills that eliminated the tedious work of turning millstones, these new electric windmills made life easier, too.

Explorer Rear Admiral Richard Byrd took a Jacobs wind generator to the Antarctic in the 1930s, and it ran for twenty-two years without any repairs. It only stopped working when the snowdrifts grew so high that the propellers couldn't turn anymore.

Charles Brush, a wealthy inventor and manufacturer of electrical equipment, built this giant windmill in 1888. He used it to generate power for 350 electric lights in his mansion. A huge battery room in the basement held 408 battery cells—glass jars filled with chemicals that stored electricity generated by the wind. Brush's wind turbine was successful but very expensive. *Western Reserve Historical Society, Cleveland, Ohio*

The New Deal but Not for Windmills

In the 1930s, President Franklin Roosevelt devised the New Deal to bring America out of the Great Depression. Thousands of businesses had failed following the stock market crash of 1929. From bankers to factory workers to farmers, millions of people lost their jobs.

Roosevelt wanted to put the country back to work and started massive public works projects to give people jobs and improve their lives. One of his New Deal plans was the Rural Electrification Project, which brought electric power lines to remote farms and ranches. This meant the end of most generating windmills in the American West.

In 1934, when Roosevelt's New Deal was getting started, an engineer named Palmer Putnam wanted to find a cheaper way to generate electrical power on a large scale. Most of our electricity was generated by burning fossil fuels. (Today, this remains true.) Before these fuels can be burned, they have to be mined or pumped and then refined before they are transported thousands of miles by fossil-fuel-burning ships, trains, or trucks to a destination where they can be converted into energy. All these costs increased Putnam's electricity bill.

Wind power was an intriguing alternative to Putnam. Wind can generate power where you find it, when you find it—and this fuel is free. So Putnam put together a team of experts in electricity, aerodynamics, engineering, and weather to build the biggest windmill ever. They called it the *Smith-Putnam wind turbine,* and they installed it on a hill called Grandpa's Knob near Rutland, Vermont, in 1941.

The Smith-Putnam turbine weighed 250 tons and sat atop a 110-foot tower. The two blades measured 175 feet in diameter. For eighteen

This 1941 photograph shows Palmer Putnam's 250-ton generating windmill being installed in southern Vermont. It was a bold experiment to harness the wind. However, a bearing failed in 1943 and it was shut down until the end of World War II. *Paul Gipe and Associates*

In the early 1900s, isolated farms in the American West relied on small windmills like this one to generate electricity for lights and perhaps a radio. *Paul Gipe and Associates*

Hairline cracks developed in Putnam's eighty-foot steel blades during the 1943–45 shutdown. Soon after it was restarted following World War II, a blade broke off and the project was abandoned. *Paul Gipe and Associates*

months the huge turbine whirled in the Vermont wind and generated electricity that fed into central power lines. Then a bearing failed in 1943 and the machine was shut down.

During this time, World War II was raging in Europe and the Pacific. American industry concentrated on building planes, battleships, and weapons for the war effort. So the enormous windmill in Vermont stood idle for two years. The huge blades were locked in place, and the vibrations from the wind caused hairline cracks on the blades. The engineers knew the blades should be repaired but started the wind turbine again in 1945 before the repairs were done. Three weeks later one of the giant blades broke off and crashed to the ground.

Putnam couldn't raise the money to continue the wind power experiment. The U.S. government decided to develop nuclear power, not knowing the dangers of radioactive contamination it carried. At the same time, oil and coal continued to provide cheap, reliable power. So the giant windmill on Grandpa's Knob faded from memory. By 1950, most American windmill companies had gone out of business.

The 1950s and 1960s were prosperous times for the United States and Europe, and people's demand for electricity increased. By 1970, one historian predicted "the twentieth century has witnessed the final decline of the windmill."

Windmills were not dead yet however; this comment was a bit premature. Mark Twain, after seeing a death notice for himself in a local paper, remarked that "rumors of my death have been greatly exaggerated." So it was with windmills. A few years later windmills returned with a new look, a new purpose, and more promise than ever.

MAKE AN ELECTRIC INVENTORY OF YOUR HOUSE

One hundred years ago most people didn't have electricity in their homes. When their houses were finally wired, they installed electric lights. Other inventions came later. Today we depend on electricity for dozens of activities.

Goal *Discover all the ways you use electricity by making an electrical survey of your home.*

Materials

Notebook

Pencil

Directions

Make a chart in your notebook like the one shown below.

Household Electric Inventory

Room	Electrical Equipment	How Often Used	Importance
kitchen	refrigerator	24 hours/day	necessity
	garbage disposal	3 times/day	convenience
	12 lightbulbs	6 hours/day	more important at night
	ventilator fan . . .		

Walk through each room of your house and write down everything that uses electricity. Look carefully—some items may be stored in cupboards and closets. Remember to include battery-operated watches, toys, and so on. (Be sure to ask permission to inspect other people's rooms first.) Don't forget the garage and the basement. What about heating and cooling systems for your house? Are they electric? Do they use electric fans or starter motors? Ask your family to help estimate how much time they use each electrical item. Some are used every day, all the time (such as a refrigerator) and others may be used only once a month (such as a Crock Pot). Mark down their answers next to each item.

During a day at home, record on another sheet of paper each time you use something electrical. Title this "My Electric Inventory" chart. Mark down each item and how many times you use it. This includes looking at an electrical watch or a clock, answering the telephone, and counting all the lightbulbs that are on in the rooms you enter.

At the end of the day, review the electrical equipment you used. Rewrite your "My Electric Inventory" chart in your notebook, putting the items in three categories: Necessity, Convenience, or Luxury. (Be certain to leave room for one more column for the next activity.) Now add all the electrical equipment from your first list that you didn't use on your inventory day.

How did your actual use compare with your estimated use? Could you live without many of your electrical items? In the next activity you'll have a chance to try.

LEARN WHAT LIFE WAS LIKE BEFORE ELECTRICITY

Some electrical inventions have been around for a long time, such as lights and radios. Others were not invented when your parents were children, such as computers. Perhaps they heard stories from *their* parents and grandparents about how people lived without any electrical equipment.

Goal *Research the past and discover old ways of doing things.*

Materials
Notebook
"My Electric Inventory" chart from previous activity
Pencil

Directions

Add an "alternate" column to your "My Electric Inventory" chart. Show the list to your parents, grandparents, and other adults. Ask them how people did things without the electrical equipment you found in your house. Write their responses in this column. Try to discover a nonelectrical alternative for everything on your list. You might remember books you've read or movies you've seen about life long ago.

Discuss all your alternatives with your family or classmates. Did you find alternatives for everything? How did the alternatives make people's lives different from yours? Was life better in any way? Was it worse? Which electrical inventions would you miss most? Which would you not miss very much?

SPEND A DAY WITHOUT ELECTRIC POWER

Plan this activity when you don't have school, so you can spend the whole day without electricity. Talk to your family about doing this activity together so that you'll experience the full impact of using no electricity around the house. Even if they don't all agree to do it, do your best to stay away from those watts! (Note: Leave your electric refrigerator or freezer running, or the food will begin to spoil. But try to eat food that needs no refrigeration.)

Goal *Experience what life was like before electricity.*

Materials
Notebook
Pencil

Directions

Spend a day without using electric power. Unplug your electric clock the night before you do this activity and take off your battery watch. (Remember, battery-powered items use electricity, even though they're not plugged into a wall socket.) Use a windup clock or watch, or try to tell time by the sun. Pay attention to everything you do. Don't turn on the lights and don't cook toast in the toaster. Try not to eat food from the refrigerator. (Discuss this with your parents first.)

Keep a diary during the day. Write about everything you do. Was it fun or hard work? Did it take longer to accomplish tasks without electricity? Which ones? Choose some non-electrical activities for part of the day—playing sports, riding your bike, or reading by daylight. See how many nonelectrical alternatives you can use (see "Learn What Life Was Like Before Electricity"). Bake cookies (if you have a gas oven) using a hand beater. Wash the dishes by hand. Try some hand sewing. (See the activities in Chapter 5). Do some household chores without electricity. Wash your clothes by hand and hang them out to dry or clean your room without a vacuum cleaner.

What can you do after dark without electricity? Will you go to bed at sunset or light candles? (Check with your parents about using candles safely.) Make your own music or tell your own stories instead of listening to a radio or watching television. Play nonelectronic games, such as checkers or chess.

On the following day, discuss with other members of your family who participated in this activity how the day went. Write down everyone's answers to the following questions: Was it hard to live without electricity for a day? What parts were the most fun? Most difficult? Could you live comfortably without electricity for very long? How would your life change if you did? What things would be better? Worse?

In the next chapter, you'll learn to measure the electricity your family uses and find ways to conserve, or use less, electricity.

CHAPTER EIGHT

Windmills Today

Back in the 1970s a few people who were worried about pollution and oil shortages began to look for new sources of energy and found an old one–wind power. No one expected the wind to run factories like it did in the Netherlands long ago. They wanted the wind to generate electricity for industry, homes, and even cars.

These new wind machines had a new name–wind turbines–and by 1995, more than twenty-six thousand wind turbines generated six billion kilowatt-hours (six terawatt-hours) of electricity throughout the world. The number of wind turbines is expected to increase by about 72 percent by the year 2000, but the electricity they will generate should increase by approximately 233 percent because new turbines are bigger and more efficient than older ones.

Is wind a good energy source for generating electricity? Yes!

But this answer also brings up more questions. How reliable is the wind? How reliable are wind turbines? How much does wind-generated electricity cost? Is it easy to add more turbines in the future? And a crucial question that concerns us today–what is the environmental value of wind energy?

What's New In the Wind

Wind technology has changed a lot since the 1970s. Inventors and engineers have experimented with different materials. They have changed the number and shape of the blades, invented new generators and controllers, tried many different-sized turbines, and added electronic components. Learning from their trials and errors, they have created strong, reliable turbines.

In past centuries the Dutch and the English didn't use the same type of windmill sails. In the 1800s, not all American ranchers agreed on the

Transformers link up to substations that send electricity on overhead lines to homes, offices, and factories. *Paul Gipe and Associates*

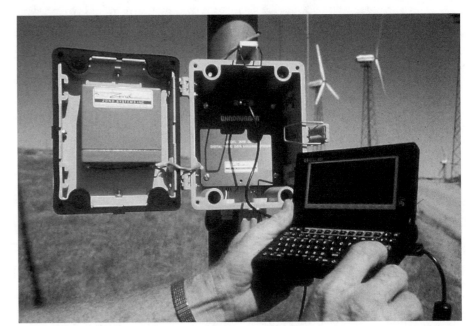

A computer attached to the wind turbine tower connects to a central office and keeps track of each turbine. It makes sure the turbine is sending a constant current through the wires. It also records how much electricity is being produced, how fast the blades are spinning, how hot the generator is, and how fast and what direction the wind is blowing. *Zond Corporation*

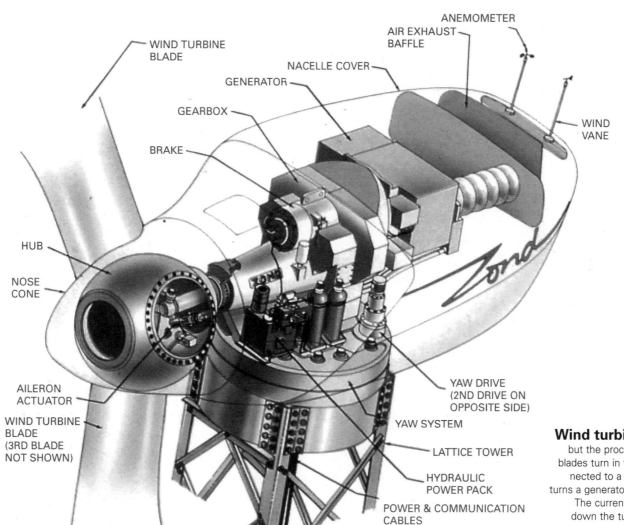

WIND TURBINE
BLADE

ANEMOMETER

AIR EXHAUST
BAFFLE

NACELLE COVER

GENERATOR

GEARBOX

BRAKE

WIND
VANE

HUB

NOSE
CONE

AILERON
ACTUATOR

WIND TURBINE
BLADE
(3RD BLADE
NOT SHOWN)

YAW DRIVE
(2ND DRIVE ON
OPPOSITE SIDE)

YAW SYSTEM

LATTICE TOWER

HYDRAULIC
POWER PACK

POWER & COMMUNICATION
CABLES

Wind turbines have many parts, but the process is fairly simple. The blades turn in the wind. They are connected to a drivetrain, or shaft, that turns a generator that makes electricity. The current is sent through cables down the turbine tower and underground to a transformer. *Zond Corporation*

Both blades and nacelle, or body, are made of fiberglass cloth and polyester resin to withstand heavy winds for many years. Two sensors in the back measure wind speed and direction. This information is sent to a computer in the nacelle that triggers a motor to keep the blades turned in the direction of the wind. When the wind becomes too strong, the computer stops the rotor. *Zond Corporation*

best windmill design. The same is true today. For example, all wind turbines operate within a certain wind speed range, from about seven mph to about fifty-five mph. Under seven mph, the rotors don't turn fast enough to generate electricity. Above fifty-five mph the wind can damage certain turbines, so they are shut down.

Different turbines slow the rotors in different ways before applying a brake. Many models feather, or turn, the angle of the blades when the wind is too strong. Feathered blades catch less wind and slow down. But some Danish turbines have blades that can't feather. At about fifty-five mph, the flow of wind over the blades becomes less productive and the rotor automatically sheds power. Two different turbines offer two different solutions to the same problem, and both do the job.

A turbine needs to run at a constant speed to produce a constant flow of electrical power. The generator regulates this flow. However, when the wind falls below a certain speed, the generator cannot maintain a constant flow and shuts down. A variable-speed generator can increase the range of wind speeds that a turbine can operate under by switching gears when wind speed changes. Other turbines solve the wind speed problem by having two generators in each turbine—one that works at lower wind speeds and one that works when the wind is stronger. Again, both types of turbines solve the problem of varying wind speeds.

Most wind turbines are the propeller type. Set high on a tower, these machines do not disturb grazing cattle or wildlife who live beneath them. Wind farm companies pay ranchers and farmers for the wind rights on their land. *Zond Corporation*

Like the old Dutch windmills, contemporary wind turbines come in different sizes. Models with rotor diameters as small as 5 feet are sold to rural homeowners to generate power in their own backyard. A few giant experimental models with rotors 200 to 300 feet in diameter have been installed. However, the most popular and most economical are medium-sized turbines with rotors about 50 to 120 feet in diameter that produce fifty to five hundred kilowatt-hours of electricity. The rotors on the old Dutch windmills stretched up to 80 feet in length. In general, wind turbines of the same size today produce ten times the power of the old Dutch mills.

The Darrieus or "eggbeater" windmills are installed on the ground, making them easy to inspect and repair. They also accept wind from any direction. *Paul Gipe and Associates*

MEASURING ELECTRICAL POWER

A (amps) x V (volts) = W (watts)
100W lightbulb burning 30 minutes uses 50W hours
100W lightbulb burning 1 hour uses 100W hours
1,000W = 1 kW (kilowatt)
1 kW x 1 hour = 1 kWh (kilowatt-hour)
1,000,000W x 1 hour = 1 MWh (megawatt-hour)
1,000,000,000W x 1 hour = 1 TWh (terawatt-hour)

Your family's electricity bill shows how many kWh you
  use.
Utility plants measure power in megawatts.
The annual production of wind farms is measured in
  TWh.

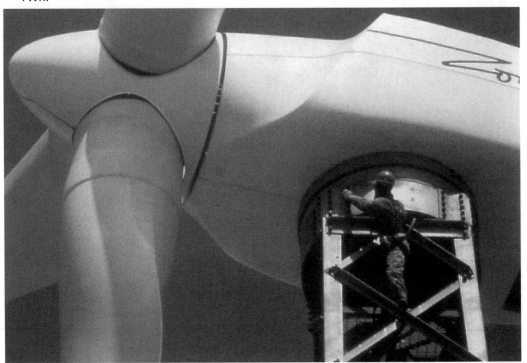

Modern windmillers, called *windsmiths*, perform regular checkups on turbines to replace parts before they wear
out. They work in all kinds of weather—desert heat, mountain storms, and high winds. *Zond Corporation*

How Well Does Wind Power Work?

A wind turbine can be evaluated in two ways. First is *availability*–how much of the time a machine is in working order. With a good, regular maintenance program, a wind turbine will be ready to work more than 95 percent of the time. This is as good or better than fossil fuel or nuclear power plants.

The second measurement is called the *capacity factor*–how much time the turbine is generating electricity. Here is where wind power lags behind, for as windmillers have always known, the wind can be intermittent. Coal or oil will always burn, but the wind won't always blow. Nevertheless, the capacity factor of wind turbines has increased from 15 percent in 1980 to 35 percent today. The wind isn't blowing harder now, but engineers know how to capture more wind.

The wind blows strongest on the top of smooth, rounded hills, across open plains, near shorelines, and between mountain gaps. Hills, woods, lakes, and other landscape features affect wind speed. Turbines themselves change wind patterns. If turbines are placed in straight rows on flat ground, the ones in front grab the most wind, and those in back lose out. Even on hillsides, turbines placed too close together can steal each other's wind.

Wind speed is more predictable than rainfall, but years of wind drought are not uncommon. *Wind farm* companies track the wind for several years before installing turbines. Placing turbines on the best sites to capture the most wind means that the machines will be more productive, more electricity will be produced, and wind-powered electricity will become more and more cost effective.

But wind speed is only one thing to consider. Does the area get hit by tornadoes? Hurricanes? Ice storms? Any of these conditions can damage wind turbines, increase repair costs, and decrease the amount of time that the turbines are operational.

Is there a finished road leading to the site? If not, is it possible to build one or is the site only accessible to mountain goats? Building and maintaining roads is expensive.

How close are the electricity transmission lines needed to transport this power to those who need it? Wind turbines can generate electricity, but this must be accessible to the people who need it. Building long-distance power lines can cost more than the turbines themselves.

What Does Wind Power Cost?

A well-placed wind turbine can generate electricity for about six cents per kilowatt-hour. Since the fuel—the wind—is free, this cost includes the cost of the turbine and the

Many American wind turbines are mounted on open lattice towers, like the old prairie windmills. These towers are cheaper than solid towers and tend to "disappear" when you see them from a distance. They are also safer during earthquakes, an important advantage in California. *Zond Corporation*

maintenance. Most wind turbines are built to last about twenty years, so the cost of the turbine is averaged over twenty years. Installing a wind farm costs about the same as building a new fossil-fuel-powered generating station. Old coal-, oil-, and gas-powered plants are cheaper to run if you count the cost of power generation alone. However, we are paying another price for our energy that cannot be computed–an environmental price. We should consider the cost of this environmental damage when we compare wind energy to fossil fuel energy.

In Europe, people prefer the look of solid towers. Windsmiths like them, too, because a ladder inside the tower protects them from wind and rain when they climb up to make repairs. *Paul Gipe and Associates*

LEARN HOW MUCH ELECTRICITY YOU USE

Goal *Read your electric bill and meter to understand how much energy you use.*

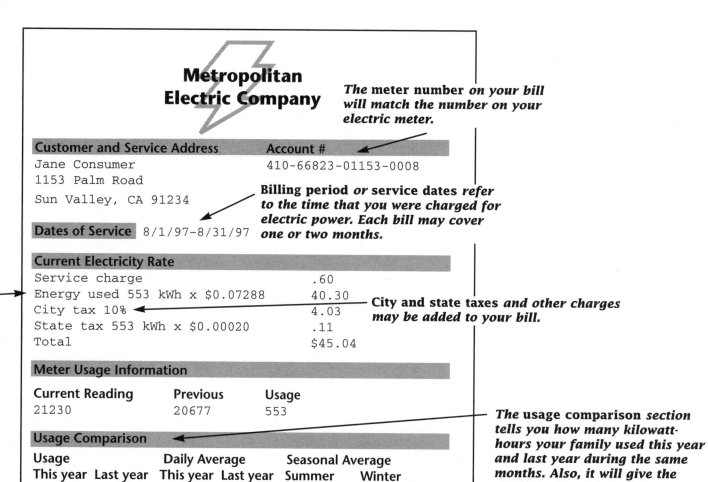

Metropolitan Electric Company

The meter number on your bill will match the number on your electric meter.

Customer and Service Address | **Account #**

Jane Consumer
1153 Palm Road
Sun Valley, CA 91234

410-66823-01153-0008

Billing period or service dates refer to the time that you were charged for electric power. Each bill may cover one or two months.

Dates of Service 8/1/97–8/31/97

Current Electricity Rate

Service charge	.60
Energy used 553 kWh x $0.07288	40.30
City tax 10%	4.03
State tax 553 kWh x $0.00020	.11
Total	$45.04

City and state taxes and other charges may be added to your bill.

Energy used or energy charged will tell you how many kilowatt-hours (kWh) you used during this time period, the basic charge per kilowatt-hour, and the total cost of your electricity.

Meter Usage Information

Current Reading	Previous	Usage
21230	20677	553

Usage Comparison

Usage		Daily Average		Seasonal Average	
This year	Last year	This year	Last year	Summer	Winter
553 kWh	699 kWh	9 kWh	12kWh	10.4 kWh	19.6 kWh

The usage comparison section tells you how many kilowatt-hours your family used this year and last year during the same months. Also, it will give the average daily use and the seasonal average for both years.

Materials

**Electric bills from the past year, one for each
season**

Notebook

Pencil

Calculator

Stool

Flashlight (optional)

Directions

Look at your family's electricity bills from the
previous year. (If necessary, you can probably
order duplicate copies from your electric company.) The categories on your bill may not
have the same names as those illustrated
above, but you should find the same information.

How much electricity—in kilowatt-hours—
does your family use each year? Find out a
daily average by taking the total monthly reading and dividing it by the number of days in
that month.

Draw a graph in your notebook, like the one
shown on the opposite page, to record your
family's use of kilowatt-hours. Mark a range of
kilowatt-hours on the vertical axis and the
names of the months on the horizontal axis. Do
you use more electricity in different seasons?
Why? Look at your list of electrical equipment
in the activity called "Make an Electric

Inventory of Your House" in the previous chapter to see what might make the difference.

Now measure how much electricity you are
using today. Find your electric meter. It may be
outside, in the basement, or in a hallway. You
may need a stool or a flashlight to see the
meter. If you live in an apartment building,
there may be many meters, one for each unit.
Check the number on the meter to see that it
matches the meter number on your electric bill.

An electric meter has a wheel in the center.
The faster the wheel rotates, the more electricity you are using at that moment. Watch how
fast the meter turns. Walk through your house
and see how many electrical items are on
(lights, television, and so on). Turn off anything
that is not needed. Look at your meter again
and see if the wheel spins more slowly.

The five dials on the meter turn at different
speeds and show the number of kilowatt-hours
used. Create a chart like the one on page 97.
Read your meter then write down the numbers
on the dials from *left to right*. Look at the one
on the extreme left. Is the dial pointing directly
to a number? Write down that number. If the
pointer is between two numbers, write down
the *lower* number. Read the dial to the right in
the same way, and record it to the right of the
first number. Continue reading the dials and

writing the numbers.

Look at your latest electricity bill. How many days have passed since the last official meter reading? What was the kilowatt-hour reading then? Subtract this amount from your reading. Is it more or less than the last billing period? Can you explain the change?

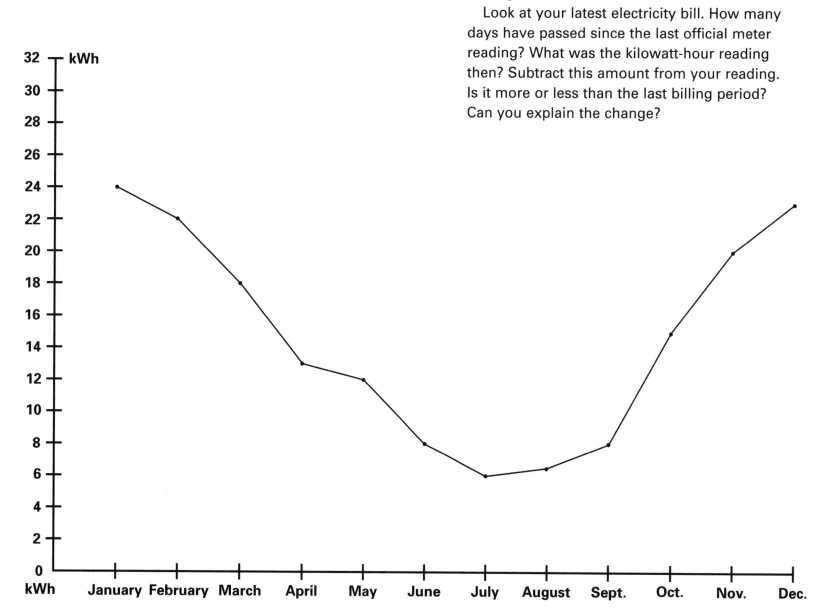

SAVE ENERGY AT HOME

Goal *Monitor your electricity use and change your energy habits to conserve electricity.*

Materials
Notebook

Pencil

Directions

Make a chart like the one below. Read your electric meter each day for a week (see page 96.) Try to determine why you used more or less electricity during different days of the week.

Call a family meeting and talk about using less electricity. Ask your electric company for information about energy conservation programs. Their phone number should be on your bill. Share these conservation ideas with your family. Create a plan for your family to modify their electricity use by doing things like turning off lights when leaving a room, turning off the television, and more. You may save a few dollars a month on your electricity bill. Each family's energy habits *do* make a difference.

After putting this energy-saving plan into action, read the electric meter each day for another week and record the results. Call another family meeting and review your findings. Are you using less electricity? Does everyone agree that you are as energy-efficient as you can be? If the answer to both questions is yes, congratulate yourselves. If you think you can be more energy-efficient, review your conservation plan and keep trying. The following ideas may help.

Date	Current Meter Reading	Previous Meter Reading	Kilowatt-hours Used	Special Activities
11/4	16698	16685	13	
11/5	16723	16698	25	portable heater on 8 hours
11/6	16739	16723	16	lights and TV on all day
11/7	16747	16739	8	away all day
11/8				
11/9				
11/10				

HINTS FOR CONSERVING ENERGY

- In the winter, lower your thermostat a few degrees to save heat and put on a sweater instead. If you use air conditioning in the summer, keep your house a few degrees warmer than usual to save energy. Do you need to heat or cool every room in the house all day long? Is it possible to close some air vents in rooms you aren't using?
- Insulate your home (walls, windows, doorways) and your hot water heater to save on heating and cooling costs. (Your power company may pay part or all of the costs of these conservation measures.)
- Turn your refrigerator dial to a warmer setting to save energy.
- Turn lights and electronic equipment off when no one is in the room.
- Don't use the heated drying setting on your dishwasher. This doubles the amount of energy it takes to do the dishes.
- Many new models of electrical equipment—including that energy hog, the refrigerator—use much less electricity than older models. When it's time to buy a new appliance or piece of electronic equipment, compare the energy use of different models. (Some appliances offer energy cost/savings charts affixed to their exterior.)
- Try compact fluorescent lightbulbs. They cost more to buy, but they use *much less* electricity and last ten to twenty times longer than ordinary incandescent lightbulbs. In the long run, they are much cheaper and more energy-efficient. Also, your electricity company may give special rebates for compact fluorescent bulbs.

Anemometers, or wind-measuring instruments, measure wind patterns for a year or more before wind turbines are installed on a site. Computer programs can also predict the wind, but are not as accurate as measuring the wind directly. *Zond Corporation*

CHAPTER NINE

Fulfilling the Promise

When you stand by the roadside one hundred feet away from a giant wind turbine, you hear a deep whoosh . . . whoosh . . . whoosh as the rotors turn. The eggbeater turbines give out a chug . . . chug . . . chug. Even louder is the sound of the wind roaring in your ears. The wind may blow off your hat and tangle your hair. It may chill you through and through. But wind energy is clean and safe–and we will never run out of it.

Environmental Price of Fossil Fuels

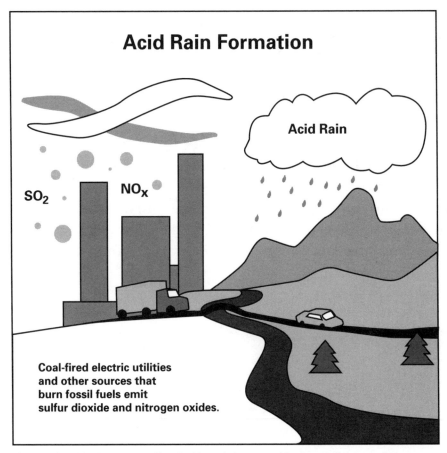

Acid Rain Formation

Acid Rain

SO_2 NO_x

Coal-fired electric utilities
and other sources that
burn fossil fuels emit
sulfur dioxide and nitrogen oxides.

Burning fossil fuels creates sulfur dioxide and nitrogen oxide. Some of these pollutants quickly fall back to earth as gases or particles. Others mix with water in the atmosphere and form acids. These acids can travel hundreds of miles before they fall to earth as acid rain, snow, or fog. Acid rain is damaging forests, rivers, lakes, and farm crops all over the world. *U.S. Environmental Protection Agency, Acid Rain Division*

Fossil fuels—coal, oil, and natural gas—have become our main sources of energy. Burning fossil fuels generates electricity, heats homes, and runs cars, trucks, and airplanes. However, these fuels also cause acid rain, air and water pollution, and global warming.

Acid rain forms when gases from burning fossil fuels mix with water vapor in the atmosphere. Falling to earth, acid rain poisons plant and animal life in fields, forests, and lakes. Emissions from car exhausts and factory smokestacks react with sunlight to form smog. Smog can bring about serious health problems such as asthma and other respiratory illness, heart disease, and cancer.

The vast quantities of fossil fuels that we burn add excess carbon dioxide to the atmosphere, which traps the sun's heat and raises global temperatures. Many scientists believe that this global warming may already be causing widespread climate changes. If their predictions come true, farmland may become desert, violent storms may cause widespread destruction, and melting polar ice caps may flood coastal regions all around the world—all within a single lifetime. The human suffering caused by such disasters would touch everyone.

The Environmental Price of Power

Fossil fuel power plants produce low-priced electricity–if you don't count the hidden environmental costs. But these costs are real. In human terms, a 1995 report by the American Lung Association stated that nearly two thousand deaths a year in the United States would be prevented if air pollution standards were tightened. The health damages caused by burning fossil fuels cost the American economy about $11 billion every year.

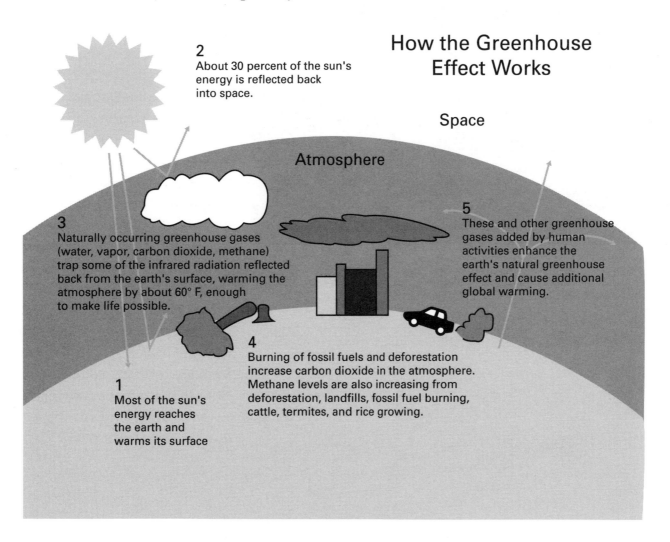

How the Greenhouse Effect Works

2
About 30 percent of the sun's energy is reflected back into space.

Space

Atmosphere

3
Naturally occurring greenhouse gases (water, vapor, carbon dioxide, methane) trap some of the infrared radiation reflected back from the earth's surface, warming the atmosphere by about 60° F, enough to make life possible.

5
These and other greenhouse gases added by human activities enhance the earth's natural greenhouse effect and cause additional global warming.

4
Burning of fossil fuels and deforestation increase carbon dioxide in the atmosphere. Methane levels are also increasing from deforestation, landfills, fossil fuel burning, cattle, termites, and rice growing.

1
Most of the sun's energy reaches the earth and warms its surface

At first glance, this forest in the Andirondack Mountains of New York looks healthy, but a closer look reveals bare white trunks among the trees. Acid rain, snow, and fog have contributed to the deaths of these high-altitude spruce trees. The acid damages leaves so they cannot produce enough food energy. Weakened trees are attacked more easily by diseases and insects that can kill them. Acid rain also dissolves nutrients in the soil and washes them away. Wildlife in lakes and rivers also have been killed by acid rain runoff. *Gary Randorf / Adirondack Council*

The natural world suffers, too. About 70 percent of the trees in the high elevations of Vermont's Green Mountains have died due, in part, to acid rain. A warmer climate in Alaska has coincided with the decline of cedar forests there. Rising sea levels in Florida are killing sabal palms along the Gulf Coast. Animal life declines as well when habitats are destroyed.

It is difficult to calculate the dollar cost of environmental damage caused by pollution. What is the value of a forest that is not clear-cut but left in its natural state? If we want to measure the cost of clean air, do we include the health care costs and lost work days of people who get sick in a polluted city? Or do we look at a clean-air city and add up the savings in health care and gained work days? If we could put a dollar value on these environmental costs and then add them to the price we pay for electricity, home heating, and transportation generated from fossil fuels, then the true cost of this energy source would be known. If we could do this, it would be clear that wind-generated power is more economical today and is a better investment for future generations.

Renewable Energy Sources

Various renewable energy sources are less polluting than fossil fuels, but they are not all environmentally harmless. Hydropower projects involve damming rivers, then using falling water to turn turbines and generate electricity. This produces no emissions but radically alters the ecology of rivers that are dammed. Burning ethanol, wood, and other biomass products reduces some pollutants but doesn't eliminate carbon dioxide emissions.

Wind and solar power are the cleanest renewable energy sources, with zero polluting emissions and virtually no ecological damage. Solar

Hurricane Hugo left behind massive amounts of wreckage in 1989. In recent years, we have witnessed an unusual number of natural disasters such as flooding, drought, and tropical storms. Many scientists believe this is due to a worldwide climate change caused by growing amounts of carbon dioxide and other greenhouse gases in the air. *National Oceanic and Atmospheric Administration Photo Library*

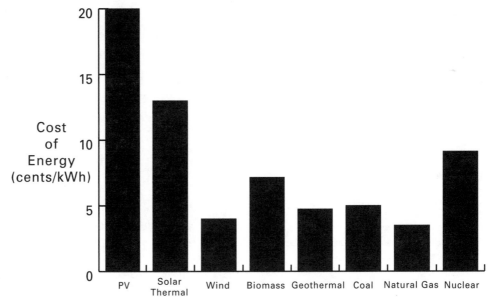

This chart shows the cost (in cents) of generating 1 kWh (kilowatt-hour) of electricity with new generating equipment. Wind energy is cheaper than many other sources. However, most of our electricity is generated by older coal and natural gas power plants that are cheaper, but much more polluting than wind turbines. *Princeton Economic Research*

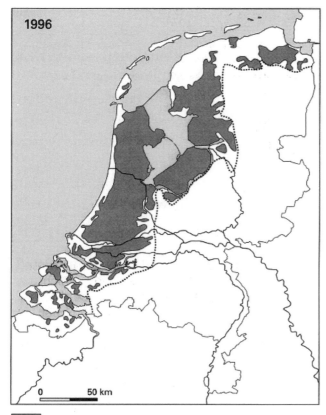

1996

land below sea level

Man-made dikes and natural sand dunes along the coast of the Netherlands still try to hold back the sea. However, the sea level is rising—another possible effect of global warming—and the dunes are constantly eroding. The Dutch government spends more than $35 million every year to replenish eight million cubic meters of sand on the beaches and dunes. They do this by sucking up sand from the sea floor into the hold of a ship, and then spraying it onto the beach. The Waterwolf appears to be snapping and biting the Netherlands more than ever before. *Information and Documentation Center for the Geography of the Netherlands*

energy has a bright future but is still rather expensive. Of all renewable energy forms, wind technology is the most advanced and most cost-effective. Wind-powered electricity costs about the same as electricity generated from new fossil fuel-burning plants (about four to six cents per kilowatt-hour) but without the additional environmental costs. The fuel for a turbine—the wind—is free. The costs of wind energy are the turbines themselves and the people who service them.

Wind Farm Opponents

Not everyone likes wind farms. Oil and coal companies and many utility companies profit from the current fossil fuel energy industry and don't want to change to renewable energy such as wind. Many of these industries influence politicians who make energy laws, so progress toward more clean, renewable energy has been slow. For example, in 1996 pressure from automakers and oil companies killed a California regulation that would have put hundreds of thousands of zero-emission electric cars on the highways by 2002. "The opposition from automakers was so strong, uniform, concerted, well-funded, and unyielding that it would have been foolhardy to proceed," said environmentalist Lynne Edgerton, a member of the California Air Resources Board.

Though some utility companies support wind energy projects, many others are urging Congress to repeal laws requiring utilities to buy some of their electrical power from small independent companies like wind farms.

Some people who live near wind farms don't like the way they look. The first California wind farms were a crowded jumble of different types of turbines. Surveys have found that people accept wind farms more easily when turbines aren't densely packed and when similar styles are grouped together.

In Great Britain, some of the windiest spots are the most beautiful. Some environmentalists, committed to preserving the wilderness, want to leave the land untouched. Other environmentalists, eager to reduce pollution, want to establish wind farms. Both groups are working to protect the environment. They are working together to reach a compromise.

Preventing Bird Kills

A few wind farms have had problems with birds' being killed by whirling rotors that spin too fast for birds to see them. For example, researchers counted 182 dead birds in two years from the 6,500 wind turbines in Altamont Pass, California. Though this loss of wildlife is not acceptable, it is far less than the estimated 57 million birds killed each year by airplanes and other vehicles. Oil spills are another catastrophe for birds. Thirty thousand dead birds were counted and as many as 300,000 may have died in the Exxon *Valdez* oil spill in 1989. Even if wind turbines continued to kill birds at the present rate, it would take one thousand years to kill as many birds as the Exxon *Valdez*. However, the wind energy industry will not let this happen. An environmental task force has been organized by leading companies in the U.S. wind industry and the American Wind Energy Association. It has brought together bird specialists to study bird behavior, turbine design, and turbine placement to protect birds in Altamont Pass and other wind farm sites.

Small wind turbines bring clean, low-cost electricity to villages and farms all over the world. Sometimes a combination of a wind turbine and photovoltaic solar panels works together to provide steady power when the wind doesn't blow or the sun doesn't shine. *Paul Gipe and Associates*

Bird specialists working with wind turbine companies are exploring ways to prevent birds from colliding with turbine blades. Striped blades help to keep birds away. *Kenetech Windpower, Inc.*

A scientist is testing a cable strung across the tower to discourage birds from perching near the whirling blades. *Kenetech Windpower, Inc. / Lindsay Wildlife Museum*

In one project, researchers are putting transmitters on golden eagles to track the birds' movements. Scientists study bird populations at proposed turbine sites to avoid busy flyways and nesting and hunting areas. Clear flyways are created on wind farms to accommodate migrating birds. Radar can also track flight activity and shut down turbines if birds get too close.

Dr. Tom Cade, chairman of the task force says, "I'm convinced we're moving in the right direction for the environment, for wildlife, and for wind energy. I'd like to think that this research will result in a situation in which everybody emerges as a winner."

How Much Wind Power Could We Use?

Wind energy is a promising but minor player on the energy team today. With the proper coaching, it could be a much stronger player. In 1990, less than one-tenth of 1 percent of our energy was generated from wind power, but wind power *could* supply 20 percent of electricity in the United States in the next few years. That's two hundred times more than we generated in 1990, and it would save 900,000 tons of fossil fuels from going up in smoke each year. Not all areas are windy enough for wind farms, but vast resources in the northeast, midwest, and western United States are waiting to be tapped.

Major Obstacle to Using Wind Power

How can we fulfill the promise of wind power? Some technical problems need to be solved. Engineers and scientists are working to find ways to store surplus electricity to use when the wind isn't blowing. They are looking for ways to improve wind turbines even more.

The major obstacle to wind energy development in North America is lack of official support. Federal and state governments have given enormous financial aid to fossil fuel and nuclear power industries since their inception. If renewable energy received the same support, we would see many more wind farms all across the continent.

Environmental groups are working worldwide to alert people about the threat of global distress and the promise of renewable energy. They are trying to convince people to put pressure on national governments to change energy policies *before* our environmental problems become irreversible. The problems are near at hand, but so are the solutions.

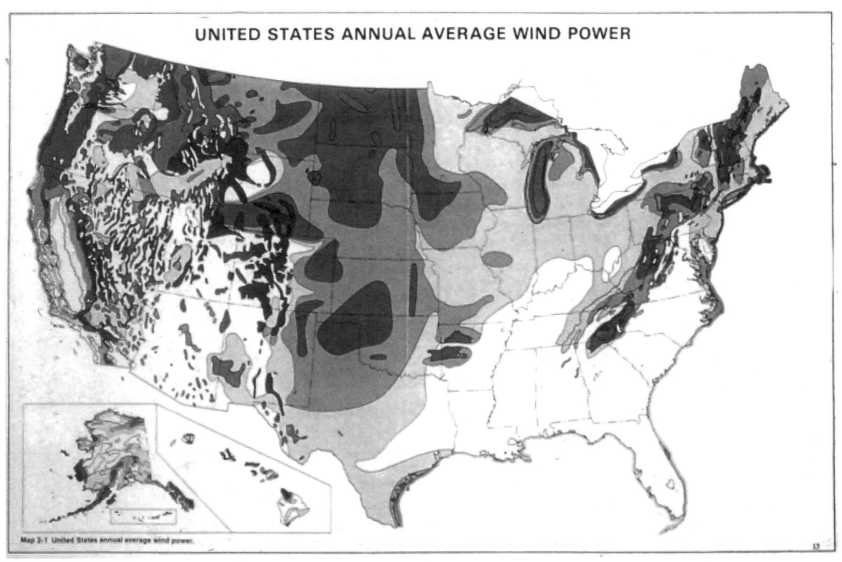

The wind blows strong enough in many parts of the United States to generate 20 percent of our electricity using wind power. The areas that are dark and shaded offer the best sites for wind farms. The Great Plains are especially breezy, as early pioneers discovered. Other windy areas include coastal regions, the Great Lakes region, and mountain ranges. *National Renewable Energy Laboratory*

Dozens of electrical utility companies across the United States have conducted surveys among their customers. These surveys show that American families are very concerned about environmental pollution and that they are willing to pay more for electricity generated by clean, renewable energy sources. Now it's up to lawmakers and utility companies to provide these consumers with the clean power they want.

Wind Power around the World

Wind technology is an environmentally friendly and economical form of energy that we can use to help meet our current energy needs and heal our planet. *Zond Corporation*

Europe has moved ahead of the United States in wind power development. In 1985, the United States produced 90 percent of all wind-generated electricity. By 1995, it produced only 34 percent. European countries are installing many new turbines every year while the United States continues to fall further behind.

Denmark, the early pioneer of wind-powered electricity, has officially adopted a goal to use wind power to generate 10 percent of its electricity by the year 2000. Many Danish families pool their money to buy wind turbines. They also vote for candidates who favor the development of wind energy. Five of the seven political parties in Denmark have formed a green coalition that promotes official government support of wind energy policies. Germany and the Netherlands also have growing wind technology industries.

Wind power makes sense for developing countries, too. Plentiful wind is found in more parts of the world than fossil fuels. India has one of the largest wind energy industries in the world today. Developing countries are using a mix of energy sources on a small scale. Some wind turbines are connected to solar panels or diesel generators to produce electricity when the wind doesn't blow. One or two wind turbines can provide enough electricity for an entire village. As the village economy grows, more turbines can be added.

Winds of Change

The power of the wind has created many environmental changes over the centuries. The Dutch and their windmills drained and enlarged their country. North American windmills helped to transform the American desert into the breadbasket of the world.

Today, the power of the wind is perhaps more important than ever before. Modern wind machines can help to fill our energy needs with clean, safe power, and they may help to save our planet. That means there's good news in the wind.

Zond Corporation

SEE THE EFFECTS OF ACID RAIN

This experiment will test the effects of acid rain on the growth of seeds over a seven-day period. You will attempt to sprout two crops of alfalfa seeds: one with water and one with acid rain.

Goal *Learn about the effects of acid rain.*

Materials
Notebook

Pen

4 ounces alfalfa seeds (available at health food stores)

2 1-quart glass jars

Flat-bottomed strainer *or* 3-inch-square piece of fine screen

Gallon plastic container with lid

Water

Vinegar

Masking tape

Measuring spoons

Days	Jar 1: Water	Jar 2: Acid rain
Day 1		
Day 2	A few seed covers splitting	
Day 3	Some sprouting	
Day 4	Half of seeds sprouting	

Directions

Read through the experiment and formulate a hypothesis—what you think the results will be—for each of the 2 jars. Write it in your notebook. The experiment will prove or disprove your hypothesis.

Label the 2 quart jars with masking tape as follows: "Jar 1 Water" and "Jar 2 Acid Rain."

Fill plastic jug with water. Mix in 4 tablespoons vinegar. Vinegar is acidic. This mixture of water and vinegar matches the acid levels of the rain that falls in some areas. Label the bottle "Acid Rain—Do Not Drink" and store in a safe place.

Measure 2 tablespoons alfalfa seeds into each jar. Fill Jar 1 half full with tap water. Fill Jar 2 half full with acid rain. Soak seeds in both jars overnight. The next morning, hold the strainer or screen flat against the mouth of Jar 1 to keep the seeds from falling out. Strain all the water into a sink. Place your hand on the mouth of the jar, turn the jar on its side, and shake it to distribute seeds evenly along the side. Lay jar on its side and place it somewhere out of direct sunlight. Do the same with Jar 2.

Keep a journal of sprouting activity for each jar with a chart like the one shown at left.

Twice a day, cover the seeds in Jar 1 with tap water. Immediately strain the water into the sink using the screen and your hand to protect the seeds. Shake the jar to redistribute the seeds. Replace the jar in its former place. Do the same with Jar 2, *except rinse with the acid rain solution instead of water*. Follow this procedure for both jars for 7 days. If you run out of the acid rain solution, mix another batch combining 4 tablespoons of vinegar with a gallon of water.

After 7 days, describe the results from each of the sprouting jars in your journal. Review your hypothesis. Explain in a few sentences why you think your hypothesis was correct or incorrect. What can you hypothesize about the effects of acid rain in the natural world? What additional experiments could you do to test your hypothesis? Would it be harder to control your experiment in nature? How could you overcome these difficulties?

TAKE ENVIRONMENTAL ACTION

You can do your part to make sure that wind turbines and renewable energy fulfill their promise in the future. You'll need to use the telephone and perhaps the library in this activity to locate information about the community in which you live.

Goal *Increase your environmental awareness by doing some investigative research on your local community.*

Materials
Paper
Pen
Telephone
Library (optional)
Telephone book

Directions

Call the public affairs or community relations department of your local electrical utility company and ask them how and where your electricity is generated. It may be all from one source and one location. If it comes from several different sources, ask what percentage comes from each source.

Look at the wind map on page 110. If you live in a windy area, ask your utility company if they would be willing to buy electricity from a wind farm. Find out if there are any plans to develop wind farms in your region. The American Wind Energy Association can help you. Write to them at AWEA, Center for Renewable Energy and Sustainable Technology, 122 C Street N.W., 4th floor, Washington, D.C. 20001, or call them at (202) 383-2500.

Is your area suffering environmental damage from acid rain, air pollution, or climate changes? Check the local newspapers in the library for past articles on local environmental problems. Interview several people—your parents, neighbors, teachers, or librarians—to find out if they know of any reports about such conditions.

Find out what groups are working on your local environmental problems. Check the telephone book under "Environmental Organizations." Call and ask about their activities. Do they talk to school classes? Can students help with any ongoing community action projects? What other ways can you help? If you can't find a local group, write to a national environmental organization (see the list of environmental groups in the resource listing) to find a group that is working in your area. Perhaps you can help start a local chapter.

Write a letter to your congressional and state representatives and ask them about energy bills that are coming up for a vote. Your librarian can give you their names and addresses. Ask if they vote for or against energy bills that support renewable energy like wind power. Ask them how they vote on other environmental protection bills. Let them know that you support wind power and other environmental measures.

Where to Find Windmills

To understand the old European windmills, you should see the mighty sails turn and the giant gears mesh. You should watch the heavy millstones grind and climb to the upstairs to feel the whole mill vibrate from the force of the wind as the sails flash by the window.

To know a Western windmill, you should hear the rattle of the wind in the vanes and the clatter of the pump as it raises water from deep in the earth.

To appreciate a modern wind turbine, you should stand beneath one to feel the wind rush through your hair and hear the deep whirring as the powerful blades turn in the wind.

Here's a list of various types of windmills that are open to the public in the United States, Canada, England, and the Netherlands. For more information on a particular mill, contact the local visitor information office, chamber of commerce, or town clerk.

EUROPEAN WINDMILLS

The following old postmills and smock mills have been restored and some are still grinding grain. Some give tours only during the summer or by request. Many have museums or exhibits attached.

United States

CALIFORNIA

San Francisco
Golden Gate Park, (415) 666–7200
Two tower mills built in 1902 and 1905 pumped water to irrigate the sand dunes that became the lush gardens of Golden Gate Park.

ILLINOIS

Geneva
Fabyan County Forest, (708) 232–2631
Working Dutch smock mill.

Golden
Golden Windmill, (217) 696–4819
Smock mill in the northern German style. Museum tells the history of the mill.

Peotone
Rathje Windmill, (815) 932–0146
Smock mill recently restored by local historical society as a working mill.

IOWA

Elk Horn
(712) 764–7472
Working 1848 windmill brought from Denmark and restored in 1970s. A video and tour give information on the history of the mill.

KANSAS

Hillsboro
Hillsboro Heritage Park, (316) 947–3775
The park contains an original adobe house built by Mennonite settlers along with a barn, shed, water-pumping windmill, and a reconstructed Dutch-style grinding mill.

Smith Center
Old Dutch Mill, Wagner Park, (913) 282–3895
Open all year.

Wamego
Schonhoff Windmill, Wamego Park, (913) 456–2040
Museum and mill.

MARYLAND

Cambridge (Lloyds)
Spocott Windmill, (410) 228–7090
Restored postmill with miller's house and schoolhouse. Spocott Windmill Day held first Saturday of May.

MASSACHUSETTS

Cape Cod has the largest collection of restored European windmills in the United States. Most are open spring through fall and by appointment in the winter.

Brewster
Old Higgins Farm Windmill, Drummer Boy Park, (508) 255–7045
Working smock mill.

Chatham
Rink Windmill, Chase Park, (508) 945–5199
Near the center of town.

Eastham
(508) 255–1798
Two millers work this smock mill during the summer months. The windmill is across from the town hall and near the Visitor Center of the National Seashore.

Nantucket
Nantucket Windmill, (508) 228–1894
Working windmill grinds flour. Open spring through fall.

Orleans
Jonathan Young Mill, Town Cove Park, (508) 255–1386
Working smock mill open July and August.

Sandwich
Heritage Plantation, (508) 888–3300
A smock mill is part of the Heritage Plantation, with beautiful grounds and various historical exhibits.

Yarmouth
Judah Baker Mill, (508) 398–2231, ext. 292
Self-guided tour of smock mill.

MICHIGAN

Dearborn
Old Yarmouth Windmill, Greenfield Village, (800) 343–1929
A Cape Cod windmill that was moved to the village, a group of historical homes. Located next to the Henry Ford Museum.

Holland
De Zwann Windmill, Windmill Island, (616) 355–1030
Brought from the Netherlands and rebuilt on the island. Museum includes a miniature Dutch village with a small water-pumping windmill.

Oxford
Ludeman Windmill, (810) 628–4299
Rick Ludeman built this replica stone mill to grind flour. It is being converted into a cider press.

MINNESOTA

Grove City
Soderberg Windmill, Grove City Park, (320) 857–2322
Restored red clapboard Swedish windmill.

Mankato
Seppmann Windmill, Minneopa State Park, (507) 389–5464
Partially restored windmill made of sandstone.

NEW JERSEY

Milford
Volendam Windmill, (908) 995–4365
Working replica of a Dutch smock mill. Tours and talks about the milling process are offered during the summer.

NEW YORK

Long Island has preserved many old windmills. The following are open to the public.

Bridgehampton
Beebe Windmill, John Berwind Memorial Green, (516) 283–6011
Smock mill; southeast corner of Ocean Road and Hildreth Avenue. Operates in summer; other times by appointment.

East Hampton
Hook Windmill, (516) 324–0713
Working smock mill, open June through September, located on North Main Street.

East Hampton
Gardiner Windmill, (516) 324–0713
Newly restored to working order.

East Hampton
Pantigo Windmill, Home Sweet Home Museum, (516) 324–0713
Windmill is being restored to working condition.

Water Mill

James Corwith Windmill, (516) 726–5984
Working windmill built in 1800. Now located on the village green near a water mill and mill museum.

NORTH CAROLINA

Nags Head

Outer Banks Windmill, (919) 441–1535
Attached to a popular restaurant.

RHODE ISLAND

Jamestown

Jamestown Windmill, Windmill Hill Historic District, (401) 423–0784
District includes farms and Quaker Meeting House. Smock mill restored to working order. Located on North Main Road. Open mid-June through mid-September or by appointment.

Middletown

Boyd's Mill, Paradise Park, (401) 849–1870
Unique windmill with eight sails.

Middletown

Prescott Farm and Windmill, (401) 847–6230
Farm from 1730 with restored, working windmill.

SOUTH DAKOTA

Milbank

(605) 432–5551
Smock mill located on the outskirts of town.

TEXAS

Victoria

Victoria Grist Windmill, Memorial Park, (512) 572–2767
Restored smock mill.

VIRGINIA

Hopewell

Flowerdew Hundred Plantation, (804) 541–8897
Site of first American windmill in 1621. Archaeological sites and reconstructed buildings include working postmill.

Williamsburg

Robertson's Windmill, Colonial Williamsburg, (800) 447–8679
Working postmill.

Canada

MANITOBA

Steinbech
Mennonite Heritage Village, (204) 326–9661
A reconstructed prairie town includes a working smock mill.

ONTARIO

Bayfield
Folmar Windmill, (519) 482–7559
Working windmill that grinds grain and saws lumber. Open during the summer.

QUEBEC

Early French settlers built stone tower windmills in New France. The remains of twenty-one mills can be seen along the St. Lawrence River from Quebec City north to Rivière-Trois-Pistoles. The two listed below are restored and open to the public.

La Salle
Fleming Windmill, (514) 367–6486
Working mill and museum on the St. Lawrence River, southwest of Montreal.

St.-Louis-de-Ille-aux-Coudres
(418) 438–2184
Working stone windmill and water mill with interpretation center, located one hour north of Quebec City.

WESTERN WINDMILLS

You can see thousands of old windmills on private farms and ranches throughout the midwestern and western United States. Some are still pumping water; others are not in working order. The following Western windmills are open to visitors.

United States

ILLINOIS

Batavia
Fox River Walk, (630) 879–5235
Eight windmills are located on the river walk, all built in six local factories. Three factories, converted to other uses, still stand. The Railroad Depot Museum contains miniature windmills that salesmen used as samples.

IOWA

Audubon
Nathaniel Hamlin Park, (712) 563–3780
Contains the former County Farm with historical exhibits and eighteen reconstructed windmills.

Oscaloosa
Nelson Pioneer Farm Museum, (515) 672–2989
Pioneer farm and working windmill along with other village buildings including a general store, stagecoach office, schoolhouse, and Quaker meeting house.

Urbandale, near Des Moines
Living History Farms, (515) 278–2400
Replicas of Native North American farming settlement, 1850 pioneer farm, 1900 farm, and 1875 village. The 1900 farm has a windmill that pumps water for animals.

KANSAS

Colby
Prairie Museum of Art and History, (913) 462–4590
Restored settlement includes sod house, 1930s farmhouse, and working windmill.

Wichita
Old Cowtown Museum, (316) 264–0671
Thirty restored buildings with exhibits. Windmill stands near railroad depot.

MARYLAND

Oxon Hill
Oxon Hill Farm, (301) 839–1177
Working farm with western mill located in Oxon Cove Park.

NEBRASKA

Grand Island
Stuhr Museum of the Prairie Pioneer, (308) 385–5316
Reconstructed railroad town with museum, farm, and two windmills.

Grand Island
Windmill State Recreation Area, (308) 468–5700
Three windmills, including a large railroad mill, at this lakeside campground, located on Highway I–80 between Kearney and Grand Island.

Minden
Pioneer America Museum, (308) 832–1181
Reconstructed village with twenty-five buildings and an old western windmill.

Nebraska City
Kregel Windmill Museum Company, (402) 873–4293
Restored windmill factory with original equipment.

NEW MEXICO

Portales
Windmill Collection, (505) 356–6263
Bill Dalley has restored seventy-five windmills that are displayed behind his house. This collection is open to the public.

TEXAS

Canyon
Panhandle-Plains Historic Museum, (806) 656–2244
"Windmills of the West" exhibit with artifacts and photographs. T-Anchor Ranch House and windmill reconstructed on the grounds.

Lubbock

National Ranching Heritage Center, Museum of Texas Tech University, (806) 742–2498

More than thirty old ranch buildings and four historic windmills.

WISCONSIN

Cassville

Stonefield Historic Site, (608) 725–5210

Homestead site, 1890s village, and windmill located in Nelson Dewey State Park.

Canada

ALBERTA

Etzikom

Etzikom Museum and Canadian Historical Windpower Centre Museum, (403) 666–3737

Museum of pioneer days, interpretive center, and eighteen restored windmills including a replica of a 1639 European mill.

WIND TURBINES

United States

CALIFORNIA

Altamont Pass

Located on Route 580, fifteen miles east of Oakland. More than six thousand wind turbines. Traveling on the back roads will give you panoramic and closeup views.

San Gorgonio Mountain Pass

Located on Route 10, northeast of Palm Springs; 3,500 wind turbines.

Tehachapi

Tehachapi-Mojave Wind Resource Area

The Pacific Crest Trail runs through this area. You can hike for about seven miles to get a closeup view of some of the five thousand wind turbines. Self-guided tour map available from the Kern Wind Energy Association, P. O. Box 277, Tehachapi, CA 93581. Located off Highway 58.

Canada

ALBERTA

Pincher Creek
Cowley Ridge Wind Farm
Canada's largest wind farm with fifty-two turbines. Information available from the Community Information Centre, Box 2647, Pincher Creek, AB T0K 1W0, Canada.

England

Many smock and postmills are open to the public. For books and maps, write to the Society for the Protection of Ancient Buildings, 37 Spital Square, London E1 6DY, England.

Netherlands

De Hollandsche Molen, the world's oldest windmill preservation society, founded in 1927, has restored more than seven hundred windmills. Since the late 1960s, the Guild of Volunteer Millers has taught the craft of windmilling. After two years of work, an apprentice can become a licensed windmiller. Seven hundred apprentices and seven hundred millers work the old mills. Nearly two hundred of them work full-time.

More information can be obtained by contacting either the Netherlands Board of Tourism, 355 Lexington Avenue, 21st floor, New York, NY 10017, or Provinciale Molencommissie van Noord-Holland, postbus 6090, 2001 HB Haarlem, Netherlands

Zaanse Schans
A few miles north of Amsterdam; a reconstructed village with thirteen working windmills including a paint mill, grain mill, mustard mill, oil mill, drainage mill, and the only remaining paper mill. The Molenmuseum presents exhibits and elaborate models of old windmills.

Kinderdijk
Nineteen drainage mills, located a few miles from Dordrecht. A few of them are open for viewing. One working mill contains the miller's residence. A boat ride up the canal gives a close view of all the mills.

Resource Listing

RENEWABLE ENERGY AND WIND ENERGY GROUPS

Use a search engine and do a key word search on "wind energy," "windmills," or "wind turbines" for the latest news from these and other groups on the internet.

American Wind Energy Association (AWEA)
Center for Renewable Energy and Sustainable Technology (CREST)
122 C Street N.W., 4th floor
Washington, D.C. 20001
(202) 383–2500
http://www.igc.apc.org/awea/
Provides educational materials on wind energy and other renewable energy; also works to promote governmental support of renewable energy.

Canadian Wind Energy Association
3553 31st Street N.W.
#100
Calgary, Alberta T2L 2K7
Canada
(403) 289–7713
Publishes booklets and a newletter about wind energy in general and Canadian wind projects in particular.

Energy Efficiency and Renewable Energy Clearinghouse (EREC)
P. O. Box 3048
Merrifield, VA 22116
(800) 363–3732
http://erecbbs.nciinc.com
Provides materials for different educational levels.

Kern Wind Energy Association
P. O. Box 277
Tehachapi, CA 93581
(805) 822–7956
Publishes pamphlets about wind farms in California. Sponsors a wind fair each spring in Tehachapi, California.

STUDENT ENVIRONMENTAL GROUPS

Center for Environmental Education
400 Columbus Avenue
Valhalla, NY 10595
(914) 747–8200
Library of books, magazines, and videotapes for teachers and students. Staff members will provide general resources and answer questions by phone or mail.

Earth Force
1501 Wilson Boulevard, 12th floor
Arlington, VA 22209
(702) 243–7400

Kids Against Pollution
Tenakill School
P. O. Box 775
Closter, NJ 07624
(201) 784–0668

Kids for a Clean Environment
P. O. Box 158254
Nashville, TN 37215
(615) 331–7381

The Natural Guard
142 Howard Avenue
New Haven, CT 06519
(203) 787–0229

Student Environmental Action Coalition (SEAC)
P. O. Box 1168
Chapel Hill, NC 27514
(919) 967–4600
Student grassroots organization with 2,200 local chapters for high school and college students. Holds state and regional conferences and helps students organize around various environmental issues.

Youth the Environmental Sanity! (YES!)
706 Frederick Street
Santa Cruz, CA 95062
(408) 459–9344
Presents conferences, workshops, and pamplets for middle school and high school students.

GENERAL ENVIRONMENTAL GROUPS

Greenpeace U.S.A.
1436 U Street N.W.
Washington, D.C. 20009
(202) 462–1177
Among its many projects is the Atmosphere and Energy Campaign to reduce pollution and promote renewable energy.

National Audubon Society
950 Third Avenue
New York, NY 10022
(212) 832–3200
Founded in 1886 to protect birds, its agenda includes a wide range of issues including pollution, conservation, energy development, and energy use. Sponsors Audubon Adventures for Children.

National Wildlife Federation
1400 16th Street N.W.
Washington, D.C. 20036
(800) 245–5484
Concerned with wildlife preservation and a healthy environment. Sponsors programs, camps, magazines, and more for children.

Sierra Club
730 Polk Street
San Francisco, CA 94109
(415) 776–2211
Hundreds of local chapters. Works at national and local levels to promote environmental education and environment-friendly public policy decisions.

Union of Concerned Scientists
26 Church Street
Cambridge, MA 02238
(617) 547–5552
Offers brochures and school curricula on environmental issues such as global warming.

World Wildlife Fund
1250 24th Street N.W.
Washington, D.C. 20037
(202) 293–4800
Works for conservation of wildlife and habitats.

HISTORICAL ASSOCIATIONS

International Windmillers' Association
Dr. T. Lindsay Baker
P. O. Box 507
Rio Vista, TX 76093
Lovers of Western windmills. Holds an annual trade fair with a swap meet, demonstrations of windmill restoration, and tours of windmill collections.

National Register of Historic Places
800 N. Capitol Street, LL99
Washington, D.C. 20001
(202) 343–9559
Database of information on significant properties in American history. They can do a database search by type of landmark, such as windmills. And it's free!

Society for the Preservation of Old Mills (SPOOM)
670 56th Street, S.E.; #5
Kentwood, MI 49548
Many SPOOM members own old water mills and windmills and exchange news and information about their history and restoration in a quarterly newsletter. SPOOM publishes extensive lists of restored mills in the United States, Canada, and Europe.

Windmill Careers

WIND TURBINE CAREERS

The wind energy field is a growing one. There are jobs for windsmiths, mechanics, electricians, engineers, computer and electronics experts, finance and business people, and inventors.

Engineers of many kinds are working on wind turbines—electrical and mechanical engineers, as well as those specializing in power electronics and aerodynamics. A bachelor's or a master's degree in engineering is required.

Computer specialists called software engineers write software programs to monitor data from turbines. This area is called management information systems. The software engineering group works with other engineers to develop and maintain wind turbines. Computer science graduates with a bachelor's or master's degree can enter this field.

Field maintenance people, or windsmiths, need practical experience doing electrical work, good mechanical skills, and good physical fitness. They climb up and down the towers to inspect and repair the wind turbines enduring a broiling hot summer sun or icy cold winter winds. High school graduates with trade school training can qualify for this hardy work.

Manufacturing wind turbines and water-pumping windmills requires workers with good mechanical skills including machinists, lathe operators, welders, and others. High school and trade school diplomas are useful here.

WESTERN WINDMILL CAREERS

About 200,000 water-pumping windmills still operate throughout the western United States. With regular maintenance and good repair work, these windmills can last fifty years. Professional water system specialists install and repair windmills. They also drill and service wells. A high school education and on-the-job training will prepare you for these jobs.

The University of New Mexico in Las Cruces offers a two-week summer class in windmills. This is taught by the Agricultural Extension Education Department and is open to anyone who wants to learn how to install and repair windmills. This class spends part of the time in the classroom studying the design and construction of waterpumping windmills. But most of the time is spent outside taking these windmills apart and putting them back together. Farmers, mechanics, and hobbyists who restore old windmills often attend this course. Professor James Dean says that to succeed a student needs "a high school education, a desire to learn, and practice, practice, practice."

For hobbyists who would like to construct a Western windmill but don't have room for a full-sized version, Aero Manufacturing Company sells an all-metal kit to build a model seventeen inches high (P. O. Box 403, Geneva, NE 68361).

RESTORING OLD WINDMILLS

Many old European-style windmills have been restored by local historical societies (see "Where to Find Windmills"). Though the construction work is done by professional builders, volunteers often help to operate the mills. If your town has a restored windmill, perhaps you could help out on weekends or during the summer.

Glossary

acid rain: precipitation with an increased acidity created when gases from burning fossil fuels mix with water vapor

Aermotor windmill: a windmill first developed in the 1800s by Thomas Perry who conducted more than five thousand experiments to arrive at this model

anemometer: an instrument for measuring the force or speed of the wind

axis: on a windmill, a shaft around which windmill blades rotate (see also *vertical axis windmill* and *horizontal axis windmill*)

bellows: a pump that blows air through a tube; used to blow air on a fire to make it burn hotter

cracks: lines cut on a millstone to make the grain grind evenly

Darrieus windmill: (also known as an eggbeater windmill) a vertical axis windmill, designed by Georges Darrieus, installed low to the ground with two or three loops or rotors that accept wind from any direction

dike: a wall, usually made of earth, built to hold back water

dhow: an ancient sailing boat

drainage windmill: windmill that lifts water from one level to another; used to drain lowlands in England and the Netherlands; also used to regulate water levels for flood control and irrigation

Eclipse windmill: first designed in the 1850s by Leonard Wheeler, this windmill has a small side wind vane that, in a strong wind, turned the windmill wheel sideways

fantail: a round fan of small wind vanes mounted on the back of a windmill that automatically moves the large sail to face directly into the wind

fen: a low land covered partly or wholly with water

fossil fuel: coal, petroleum, and natural gas that derive from fossils that are millions of years old; energy that is produced by burning fossil fuels; a form of *nonrenewable energy*

fulling mill: a windmill used to pound woolen cloth into felt; called stink mills by the Dutch because rancid butter and urine were used in the processing of this material

global warming: a steady increase in average temperatures throughout the world caused by an increase in carbon dioxide and other gases building up in the atmosphere and attributed to burning *fossil fuels* and other industrial processes

glue mill: a windmill that processes animal hide and bones to make glue

grist mill: a mill for grinding grain

guild: in the Middle Ages, a group of men working in the same trade or craft

Halladay windmill: a windmill design that included tilting wind vanes so the wind blew through them when the wind grew too strong

horizontal axis windmill: a windmill with blades or sails attached to a horizontal axis or support and that rotates vertically; postmills, smock mills, and contemporary propeller-type wind turbines are horizontal axis mills

hulling mill: a mill that extracts the outer layer of rice and barley kernels

Jacobs windmill: a small windmill, designed by Marcellus Jacobs, that could generate four hundred to five hundred kilowatt-hours of electricity per month; popular among farmers in isolated areas in the early twentieth century

kilowatt: equal to one thousand watts

kilowatt-hour (kWh): a unit of energy that uses one kilowatt (one thousand watts) in one hour; home electricity use is measured in kilowatt-hours

mathematical windmill: name given to the windmill designed by Thomas Perry and other inventors who used scientific experiments and mathematical formulas to build stronger and more efficient machines

millstone: large, circular stone used in a windmill to grind or crush grain or other materials

millwright: a person who designs and builds windmills,

sets up machinery, and repairs windmill machinery

megawatt: one million watts; used to measure power output by individual wind turbines

nacelle: body of a propeller-type modern wind turbine

nonrenewable energy: energy from a source that is not easily replaced, such as fossil fuels and nuclear energy

oil mill: a windmill that presses oil from seeds

paint mill: a windmill that grinds pigments for paint

patent sail: a windmill sail with wooden slats like window shutters; weights inside a mill could adjust the speed of the sails by opening and closing these shutters as the wind speed changed

polder: flatland in the Netherlands that has been reclaimed from the sea and is protected by dikes

postmill: a windmill supported by a single, sturdy post with four sails revolving around it in the direction of the wind; when the wind direction changed, millers had to change the direction of the sails to face them into the wind; first seen in Europe around 1200

reef: to reduce the size of a canvas sail by rolling and tying it up with ropes

renewable energy: energy from a source that is easily replaced, such as wind power, solar power, water power, and biomass (plant products)

rotor: the rotating part of a windmill, including the blades and blade assembly

rudder: a wooden or metal plate behind the vanes of a

Western windmill that controls the direction of the vanes

sawmill: a windmill that saws logs into lumber

sawyer: a person who works in a sawmill

slodger: nickname for a person who lived in the fens or marshlands of eastern England and who fought against the windmills that were built to drain the marshes

Smith-Putnam wind turbine: huge, experimental wind turbine built in Vermont, developed by Palmer Putnam, and in operation from 1941–43

smock mill: a windmill created in the 1300s that had sails attached to the roof or cap of the mill that revolved on an outdoor track; when wind direction changed, only the sails needed to be adjusted to face into the wind; bigger, heavier, and stronger mills than the earlier postmill design

squall: a sudden, violent wind often accompanied by rain or snow

stone dresser: traveling craftsman who sharpened millstones

terawatt-hour: one billion watts; used to measure the energy production of wind farms

tower windmill: a round stone tower with windmill sails that was common in Mediterranean countries

turn wheel: a wheel located outside a mill that allows a miller to turn the sails by hand

vertical axis windmill: windmill design with blades, attached to a vertical axis or support, that rotate horizontally; includes ancient Persian windmills and modern Darrieus windmills

watt: a unit of power used to measure electrical current

Western windmill: a design incorporating many thin blades that turn in the wind and that raise water using an underground pump; first developed in the American West and now used worldwide

wind: movement of air caused by the uneven heating of the earth by the sun; air movement caused when warm air expands and rises and is replaced by cool air

wind farm: group of wind turbines clustered together; often owned and maintained by one energy development company

windmill: a machine operated by the wind with sails or vanes that drive machinery to grind, pump, or generate electricity

windmill sail: the wooden arms of a European-style windmill; also the canvas sheets that cover the wooden sails

wind turbine: name commonly used to refer to modern windmills that generate electricity

wind vane: sail of a windmill

windsmith: a person who inspects and repairs modern wind turbines

windmiller: a person in the American West who traveled from ranch to ranch installing and repairing self-operating Western windmills; a person who operates a European-style windmill that grinds grain, pumps water, and more

Picture Key to Windmills

Drainage windmill

Grist mill

Postmill

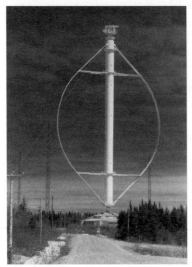

Darrieus or eggbeater windmill

Paint mill

Western windmill

134

Smith-Putnam wind turbine

Tower windmill

Smock mill

Wind turbine

Bibliography

BOOKS

Items preceded by an asterisk are written for an adult audience.

*Baker, T. Lindsay. *Field Guide to American Windmill.* Norman, Okla.: University of Oklahoma Press, 1985.

Beedell, Suzanne. *Windmills.* New York: Charles Scribner & Sons, 1975.

*Brangwyn, Frank, and Hayter Preston. *Windmills.* London: John Lane, The Bodley Head Ltd., 1923.

*Coonley, Douglas R. *Wind: Making It Work for You.* Philadelphia: The Franklin Institute Press, 1979.

Cummings, Richard. *Making Your Own Alternate Energy.* New York: David McKay Co., 1979.

*Fox, William, Bill Brooks, and Janice Tyrwhitt. *The Mill.* Boston: New York Graphic Society, 1976.

Franck, Irene M., and David Brownstone. *The Green Encyclopedia.* New York: Prentice Hall General Reference, 1992.

*Gipe, Paul. *Wind Power Comes of Age.* New York: John Wiley & Sons Inc., 1995.

*Hefner, Robert. *Windmills of Long Island.* New York: Society for the Preservation of Long Island Antiquities and W. W. Norton & Company, 1983.

Newton, David E. *Taking a Stand against Environmental Pollution.* New York: Franklin Watts, 1990.

Pringle, Laurence. *Global Warming: Assessing the Greenhouse Threat.* New York: Arcade Publishing, 1990.

——. *Rain of Troubles: The Science and Politics of Acid Rain.* New York: MacMillan, 1988.

*Singer, Charles, E. J. Holmyard, A. R. Hall, and Trevor Williams, ed. *A History of Technology, Volume II.* Oxford: Clarendon Press, 1954.

*Skilton, C. P. *British Windmills and Watermills.* London: Collins, 1947.

Spier, Peter. *Of Dikes and Windmills.* Garden City, New York: Doubleday, 1969.

*Wailes, Rex. *The English Windmill.* London: Routledge & Kegan Paul Ltd., 1954.

Weitzman, David. *Windmills, Bridges, and Old Machines.* New York: MacMillan, 1985.

MAGAZINES

Old Mill News
Society for the Preservation of Old Mills
670 56th Street, S.E.; #5
Kentwood, MI 49548
Quarterly journal of old water mills and windmills in the United States and Canada.

Windmillers' Gazette: A Journal for the Preservation of America's Wind Power History and Heritage
T. Lindsay Baker, Editor
P. O. Box 507
Rio Vista, TX 76093
Quarterly journal on Western windmill history; contains advertisements about restoring windmills.

Wind Power Monthly (U.S. Office)
P. O. Box 496007
Suite 217

Redding, CA 96049
Published in Denmark in English. Covers news of wind turbines all over the world.

VIDEOS

Historical U.S. Windmills
ECNS Video Productions
P. O. Box 819
Exmore, VA 23350
This educational video shows many of the European-style windmills all across America.

Index

Acid rain, 6, 102, 104, 115, 131

Acid rain activity, 113–14

Advertisements, 51

Aermotor Company, 66, 67–68

Aermotor windmill, 131

Aero Manufacturing Company, 130

Africa, 68

Air conditioning, 99

Airplane propellers, 78

Airplanes, 13, 107

Alaska, 68, 104

Alphonse Daudet's Windmill in Fontvielle (painting), Van Gogh, 44, 45

Altamont Pass, California, 5, 107

American Lung Association, 103

American West, 50, 68–72

American Wind Energy Association, 107, 115, 125

American windmills, 49–56, 68–72. *See also* Western windmills

Ancient wind machines, 11–14

Andirondack Mountains, 104

Anemometers, 99, 131

Antarctica, 79

Apple-cranberry cobbler (activity), 63

Arab geographers, 14

Arctic Ocean, 77

Art, landscape (activity), 45–46

Atchison, Topeka, and Santa Fe (railroad), 53

Australia, 68

Automakers, 106

Axis, 131

Baking

apple-cranberry cobbler (activity), 63

whole wheat rolls (activity), 47–48

See also Cooking

Baptizing, 72

Barbour, Erwin, 54

Batavia Historical Society, 72

Batavia, Illinois, 51

Battle-Ax windmill, 54

Beans (activity), 74

Beaufort, Admiral Sir Francis, 18

Beaufort scale, 18–20

Bellows, 13, 131

Bird kills, 107–8

Bison, 50

Blades, wood versus steel, 66–67

Bread, 39

baking (activity), 47–48

Breukelen (Brooklyn), 50

Brush, Charles, 79

Bryant, John, 39

Buffalo chips, 55

Burlington (railroad), 53

Burnham, John, 51

Byrd, Rear Admiral Richard, 79

Cade, Tom, 108

California

salt works in, 56

wind turbines in, 5, 107

California Air Resources Board, 106

Canada, 124

Canadian Wind Energy Association, 125

Cape Cod, 50, 118

Carbon dioxide, 105

Careers in windmills, 129–30

Carolinas, 50

Catholics, 44

Center for Environmental Education, 125

Cherry County, Nebraska, 55

Chicago Columbian Exposition, 67, 68

Chinese kites, 12

Civil War, 53

Climate changes, 102, 105, 115. *See also* Global warming

Coal companies, 106

Cobbler, apple-cranberry (activity), 63

Cocoa, 26

Collage, paper (activity), 57–58

Compact fluorescent lightbulbs, 99

Companies, windmill, 67–68

Computers, 88, 99, 129

Congress, letters to (activity), 115

Cooking

beans (activity), 74

corn dodgers (activity), 73

See also Baking
Corn, 14
Corn dodgers (activity), 73
Cotton gins, 55
Cow chips, 55
"Cowboy's Gettin'-Up Holler"
    (song), 74
Cracks, 41, 131
Crete, 24
Crusaders, 22
Cubitt, Sir William, 29
Customs agents, 44

Dairy farming, 47
Dangers in windmilling,
    38–39
Danish Wind Electricity
    Company, 77
Darrieus (eggbeater) wind-
    mills, 91, 131, 134
De Hollandsche Molen, 124
Deafness, 40
Dean, James, 129–30
Decorating windmills, 43, 44
Denmark, 77, 111
Denver, Colorado, 54
Deptford, England, 27, 28
Dhows, Egyptian, 11, 131
Diesel generators, 111–12
Dikes, 1, 25, 36, 106, 131
Dishwashers, 99
Drainage windmills, 25, 36,
    37, 131, 134

Drawing of windmill, 3
Dressing millstones, 41
Droughts, 54–55
Dutch. *See* Netherlands
Dutch Resistance. *See also*
    Netherlands

Earth Force, 126
Earthquakes, 93
Eclipse windmill, 51, 53, 55,
    131
Edgerton, Lynne, 106
Edison, Thomas, 67
Eggbeater (Darrieus) wind-
    mills, 91, 131, 134
Egyptian dhows, 11, 131
Egyptian windmills, 14
Electric cars, 106
Electric engines, 4
Electricity
    activities about, 83–85,
        95–99
    and Benjamin Franklin, 13
    generated by windmills,
        77–82
    measurement of, 92
    storage of, 109
Element temperatures (activ-
    ity), 7–8
Energy conservation
    (activity), 98–99
Energy costs, 105
Energy Efficiency and

Renewable Energy
    Clearinghouse, 125
Energy sources, renewable,
    5–6, 105–6, 109, 111, 132.
    See also Nonrenewable
    energy
Engines, steam, 4, 44
England
    fantails on windmills,
        28–29
    fens in, 26
    sawyers in, 27, 28
    Suffolk, 21
    windmill signaling in, 44
    windmills in, 26, 124
Environmental action (activ-
    ity), 114–15
Environmental concerns, 87,
    94, 101–12, 115
Environmental groups,
    125–27
Europe, 111
European windmills, 21–29,
    117–21
Experiments, 65–66
Exxon *Valdez*, 107

Factory-made windmills, 52,
    55
Fantails, 29, 131
Farm windmills, 54–55
Fens, 26, 131

Field maintenance, 129. *See
    also* Windsmiths
Fire hazards, 39, 40
Florida, 104
Flour, 42
Folklore of windmills, 44
Fossil fuels, 6, 80, 82, 92, 94,
    102, 106, 109, 111, 131
Franklin, Benjamin, 12–13
Fuel, 55
Fulling mills, 26, 131
Furnaces, wind, 13

Galvanizing steel, 66–67
Gasoline engines, 4
Generators, electric, 77–82
Genghis Khan, 14
Germany, 111
Global warming, 6, 102, 106,
    131. *See also* Climate
    changes
Global wind power, 111–12
Glue mills, 26, 131
Gold miners, 56
Governments, 109
Grain, 26, 42
Grain milling (activity), 30
Grand Island, Nebraska, 54
Grandpa's Knob (Vermont),
    80, 82
Great American Desert, 51,
    112

Great Depression, 80
Great Plains, 53, 54, 69, 77
Greece, 24
Green Mountains (Vermont), 104
Greenhouse effect, 103, 105
Greenpeace U.S.A., 126
Grist mills, 36, 38, 132, 134
Guild of Volunteer Millers, 124
Guilds, 27, 132
Gulf Coast, 104
Gunpowder, 26

Halladay, Daniel, 51, 65, 66
Halladay windmills, 53, 72, 132
Hanging, 72
Hazards in windmilling, 38–39
Health hazards, 40, 102, 103
Herbert, Dean, 21
Historical associations, 127
History of wind power, 1–10
Holland. *See* Netherlands
Homestead Act, 75
Horizontal axis windmills, 132
Hudson River, 50
Hulling mills, 26, 132
Hurricane Hugo, 105
Hydropower, 105

Illinois Central (railroad), 53
India, 111
Indoor plumbing, 72
Industrial Revolutions, 29
Inns, 36
Insulation, 99
International Windmillers' Association, 127
Inventors, 50–53, 65–66
Irrigation, 14, 24

Jacobs, Marcellus, 78
Jacobs Wind Electric Company, 78
Jacobs windmill, 78–79, 132
Juleff, Gill, 13

Kansas City Star, 72
Kern Wind Energy Association, 125
Kids Against Pollution, 126
Kids for a Clean Environment, 126
Kilowatt-hours, 78, 87, 92, 132
Kinderdijk, Netherlands, 25, 124
Kites, 12–13

LaCour, Poul, 77
Landscape art (activity), 45–46

Laramie, Wyoming, 53
Lattice towers, 93
Lee, Edmund, 28–29
Letters to Congress (activity), 115
Lightbulbs, 99
Lightning bolts, 39
Lincoln, Nebraska, 54
Long Island, 50

Mail-order catalogs, 54
Malt, 26
Malt mills, 46
Management information systems, 129
Manhattan, 49, 50
Mascurel, José, 6
Mathematical windmill, 65, 66, 67, 132
Measurement of electrical power, 92
Measuring wind, 99
Mediterranean islands, 24
Medlock, Frank O., 68
Megawatts, 132
Meikle, Andrew, 29
Mill at Wijk, The (painting), Van Ruisdael, 4, 45
Milling grain (activity), 30
Millstones, 2, 40, 132
  dressing, 41
Millwrights, 22, 132. *See also* Windmillers

Mine shafts, 26
Mississippi River, 51
Mongolian armies, 14
Moslem armies, 13
Mustard, 26
Mykonos, Greece, 24

Nacelle, 132
Names of windmills, 42–43, 54
Nansen, Fridtjof, 77
Napoleon, 29
National Audubon Society, 126
National Register of Historic Places, 127
National Wildlife Federation, 127
Native North Americans, 50, 51
Natural Guard, The, 126
Nebraska, 55
Netherlands, 111, 112
  dairy farming in, 47
  dikes in, 1, 25
  draining of, 24–25
  Dutch Resistance in, 44
  flag of, 43
  guilds in, 27
  map of, 25, 106
  Napoleon in, 29
  restored windmills in, 124

skating races in, 38
Waterwolf, 1, 25
windmill signaling in, 44
windmills in, 1, 4, 26
Zaan River in, 23, 29, 43
New Amsterdam, 49, 50
New Deal, 80
New York City, 49, 50
Newport, Rhode Island, 50
Nile River, 11
Nonrenewable energy, 132.
    See also Renewable
    energy
North Pole, 77
Northwestern (railroad), 53
Noyes, La Verne, 66
Nuclear power, 82, 92, 109
Nursery rhymes, 39

Oil companies, 106
Oil mills, 26, 36, 40, 132
Oil spills, 107

Paint mills, 26, 40, 132, 134
Paper collage (activity),
    57–58
Paper mills, 26, 27–28, 36
Patchwork quilts, 57
Patent sails, 29, 132
Perry, Thomas O., 65–66, 67,
    131
Persian windmills, 5, 14, 22

Phoenician sailors, 11
Photovoltaic solar panels,
    107
Pillow cover (activity), 61–62
Pioneers. *See* Settlers
Plain of Lassithi, Crete, 24
Plumbing, indoor, 72
Poisoning, 40
Polders, 25, 47, 132
Pollution, 6, 87, 102, 104, 107,
    111, 115
Postmills, 22, 39, 132, 134
Potholder (activity), 59–60
Power lines, 93
Printing presses, 55
Protestant Reformation, 44
Public works, 80
"Put his nose to the grind-
    stone," 41
Putnam, Palmer, 80, 82, 133

Quilting bee, 61
Quilts, 57

Races, skating, 38
Radio, 78
Radioactive contamination,
    82
Railroad windmills, 53
Ranchers, 54, 70. *See also*
    Farm windmills
Reef, 38, 132
Refrigerators, 99

Rembrandt van Rijn, 45, 46
Renewable energy, 5–6,
    105–6, 109, 111, 132. *See
    also* Nonrenewable
    energy
Repairs, 40, 69–70, 72
Restored windmills, 72,
    117–24, 130
Rhine River, 46
Roads, 93
Roosevelt, Franklin, 80
Rotors, 132
Rudders, 54, 133
"Rule of thumb," 41
Rural Electrification Project,
    80
Rust prevention, 66–67
Rutland, Vermont, 80

Sailboats, 2, 11
Sails, 133
    cloth, 24, 29
    patent, 29
    wooden, 29
Salt works, 56
Samson, Abbot, 21
San Francisco Bay, 56
Sandhills, 55
Sauk Center, Minnesota, 55
Sawmills, 26, 36, 49, 133
Sawyers, 27, 28, 133
Scientific American (maga-
    zine), 51

Scientific studies, 65–66
Sea levels, 24–25, 104
Sea walls. *See* Dikes
Seacoast winds, 2
Seal of New York City, 50
Sears Roebuck, 54
Seistan, Persia, 14
Settlers, 51, 53, 54, 55
Sewing (activity), 57, 59–62
"Show your metal," 41
Sierra Club, 127
Signaling by windmills,
    43–44, 72
Skating races, 38
Slodgers, 26, 133
Smeaton, John, 29
Smelting, 13
Smith-Putnam wind turbine,
    80, 82, 133, 135
Smock mills, 22–24, 46, 133,
    135
Smog, 102
Smuggling, 44
Society for the Preservation
    of Old Mills, 127
Software engineers, 129
Solar power, 105–6, 107, 111
Solid towers, 93, 94
Songs (activity), 74–76
South America, 68
Spain, 24
Squalls, 39, 133
Sri Lanka, 13

"Starving to Death on My Government Claim" (song), 75–76
Steam engines, 4, 44, 67
Steam locomotives, 53
Steam-powered sweep, 65
Steel versus wood blades, 66–67
Stink mills, 26
Stone dressers, 41, 133
Storms, 36, 38, 93
Student Environmental Action Coalition, 126
Suffolk, England, 21
Sugar cane, 14

Temperatures
  element (activity), 7–8
  and wind (activity), 9–10
Terawatt-hours, 133
Test chambers, 66
Texas, 70
Thermostats, 99
Tower windmills, 24, 133, 135
Towers
  lattice, 93
  solid, 93, 94
Toxic chemicals, 40
Transcontinental railroad, 53
Transformers, 88

Turn wheels, 36, 133
Twain, Mark, 82

Union of Concerned Scientists, 127
Union Pacific, 53
U.S. Annual Average Wind Power (map), 110, 115
U.S. Weather Service, 12, 13
U.S. Wind Engine and Pump Company, 65, 66
University of Nebraska, 54
University of New Mexico in Las Cruces, 129–30
Utility companies, 106

Valdez (ship), 107
"Valley of ten thousand windmills," 24
Van Gogh, Vincent, Alphonse Daudet's Windmill in Fontvielle (painting), 44, 45
Van Rijn, Rembrandt, 45, 46
Van Ruisdael, Jacob, The Mill at Wijk (painting), 4, 45
Vertical axis windmills, 133

Water mills, 22, 36
Waterwolf, 1, 25, 106
Watts, 133

Weather, storms, 36, 38
Weather prediction, 12, 13, 42
West. See American West
West Indies, 14
Western windmills, 121–23, 129–30, 133, 134. See also American windmills; Windmills
Wheat, 21
Wheeler, Rev. Leonard R., 51, 53
Wild West. See American West
Wildlife, 104, 107–8
Wind
  creation of, 2
  definition of, 133
  prediction of patterns, 4
Wind farms, 93, 106–7, 133
Wind furnaces, 13
Wind machines. See Windmills
Wind power
  annual average in U.S., 110, 115
  cost of, 93–94, 105, 106
  efficiency of, 92–93
  as energy source, 5–6
  and environmental concerns, 87, 101–12
  global, 111–12

  history of, 1–10
  obstacles to use, 109, 111
  opponents of, 106–7
Wind socks (activity), 15–16
Wind speed, 92–93
Wind technology, 88–91
Wind tunnels, 14, 65
Wind turbines, 87–94, 123–24, 133, 135
  Altamont Pass, 5, 107
  Brush's, 79
  careers in, 129
  design of, 90
  diagram of, 89
  production of energy by, 6
  statistics on, 87
Wind vanes, 53, 65, 133
Wind vanes (activity), 17–18
Wind-measuring instruments, 99
Windmill careers, 129–30
Windmill companies, 67–68
Windmill sails. See Sails
Windmill towers, 70, 72
Windmillers, 35–44, 133
  of the American West, 69–70
  dangers to, 38–39
  homes of, 36, 37
  See also Millwrights; Windsmiths
Windmills

in America, 49–56, 68–72
ancient, 11–14
course on, 129–30
cutaway drawing of, 3
Darrieus (eggbeater), 91,
    131, 134
decorating, 43, 44
definition of, 133
drainage, 25, 36, 37, 131,
    134
electricity generated by,
    77–82
in Europe, 21–29
factory-made, 52, 55
farm, 54–55
folklore of, 44
fulling, 26
glue, 26
grist, 36, 38, 132, 134
hulling, 26
as inns, 36
malt, 46
names of, 42–43, 54
oil, 26, 36, 40
opponents of, 27–28
paint, 26, 40
paper, 26, 27–28, 36
postmills, 22, 39, 132, 134
railroad, 53
restored, 72, 117–24, 130
sawmills, 26, 36, 49, 55
signaling by, 43–44, 72

smock, 22–24, 46, 133, 135
stink, 26
tower, 24, 133, 135
work done by, 26–27,
    55–56
See also Western windmills
Windsmiths, 92, 129, 133. *See
    also* Windmillers
Wood dust, 40
Wood versus steel blades,
    66–67
Work done by windmills,
    26–27, 55–56
World War II, 44, 82
World Wildlife Fund, 127
World's Columbian
    Exposition (Chicago), 67,
    68
Wright, Wilbur and Orville,
    13
Writing about the wind
    (activity), 31–33

XIT Ranch, 70

Youth the Environmental
    Sanity! (YES!), 126

Zaan River, Netherlands, 23,
    29, 43
Zaanse Schans, Netherlands,
    124

About the Author

Gretchen Woelfle traveled across America and to the Netherlands to visit windmills and to talk to people who restore and run them. She has published stories in *Cricket* and *Spider* magazines and writes scripts for educational CD-ROM projects. She lives with her husband and two daughters in Venice, California.